Feiteeena

Feiteceira

◆

(Portuguese Witch)

Mosqeet Mary Cardoza

iUniverse, Inc.
New York Lincoln Shanghai

Feiteceira
(Portuguese Witch)

All Rights Reserved © 2003 by Mosqeet Mary Cardoza

No part of this book may be reproduced or transmitted in any form or by any means, graphic, electronic, or mechanical, including photocopying, recording, taping, or by any information storage retrieval system, without the written permission of the publisher.

iUniverse, Inc.

For information address:
iUniverse, Inc.
2021 Pine Lake Road, Suite 100
Lincoln, NE 68512
www.iuniverse.com

ISBN: 0-595-27006-9

Printed in the United States of America

I dedicate this work to my mother, for without her lifetime of love, support and guidance, I could have made potentially disastrous choices leading to afterlife damnation.

And thanks, Ma, for making me aware and proud of my Portuguese heritage!

Contents

Introduction ix
Chapter 1   Early Exposure to the "World Beyond" 1
Chapter 2   Me, a Witch? 15
Chapter 3   Werewolf, Scott and the Ouija Board 23
Chapter 4   Witchcraft Comes Alive 29
Chapter 5   Confrontation with the Devil 35
Chapter 6   Witch Number Two and the Fortuneteller 44
Chapter 7   Not Even Death Stops Mrs. Mendes 50
Chapter 8   Angel of God, My Guardian Dear 61
Chapter 9   The Italian Stranger 63
Chapter 10   Jane Meets the "Black Cloud Mist Man." 73
Chapter 11   Signs of Trouble 77
Chapter 12   Jane Defeats the Devil 94
Chapter 13   Chicago—Dimensions Collide 108
Chapter 14   Special Gifts for the Next Generation 116

Introduction

"May you squeal like a pig on your deathbed!" Those are the curse words that open the first chapter of my incredibly true-life story.

Although these words might sound corny or clichéd, remember that corny or clichéd lines usually originated from a previously-lived event or life experience.

Let me start off by assuring you that every bizarre, supernatural, shocking experience that I've included in this story has actually happened. These are factual events!

But before you read this story, I'd like you to know that I am not on any type of hallucinogenic medication and do not suffer from mental illness. I've actually worked for a very prominent, internationally known medical/life insurance company over the past seventeen years and before that, as a third-party medical insurance biller for eight years. I am thought of by most as an organized, structured and logical person.

As my book title and name implies on the cover, my ancestors originated from Portugal, a country filled with all types of old-world traditions and superstitions. But besides their traditions and superstitions, unbeknown to most non-Portuguese, Portugal is known for its high "witch population." This story describes the origin of the "Portuguese Witch," as well as its impact to my immediate family.

My Portuguese ancestors were linked with this "witch population." And within every subsequent generation that remained in Portugal or fled to America, there is at least one that has demonstrated the "bestowed gifts," making them new "Portuguese Witches."

This person will possess the ability to prophesize, experience out of body/dimensional occurrences and encounter spiritual visitations. This person will have the tremendous responsibility of carefully choosing how to best utilize these "special gifts." Throughout their lives, they will experience first-hand both good and evil forces at work.

I know this because I am this generation's "Portuguese Witch."

My great great-grandmother, who just happened to be that generation's "Portuguese Witch," shares my name. However, this story's primary focus is on me and the extraordinary, supernatural incidents that have occurred throughout my life.

Let me provide you with a mini-preview of each chapter:

- The first chapter of this book describes the evil that surrounded my relatives in Portugal and the relatives and witches that migrated to America and settled in New England (New Hampshire and Rhode Island).

- The second chapter goes on to describe my first encounter with a self-proclaimed witch, who belonged to a witch cult in New York.

- Chapters three through six depict numerous confrontations with the devil and my first encounter with spiritual visitors.

- Chapters seven through ten describe out-of-the-ordinary dreams that came true, a message from the grave, a witch cult's continued search and an angel who diverts a potential catastrophe.

- In chapter eleven, evil entities attack and God makes himself known.

- In chapters twelve through fourteen there are more angels, evil entities attack, the devil is defeated, an inter-dimensional phenomenon occurs, and the new generation's "Portuguese Witch" is revealed.

Strangely enough, within these chapters, every phenomena encountered, from early childhood to adulthood, are linked.

The people that I met throughout my life were strategically placed for a specific purpose. A number of them have known the specific details of my life without having ever even met me. Not everyone can say they've actually met a practicing witch, talked with the devil, and been rescued by an angel.

Even though my Portuguese ancestors were given the title of "Portuguese Witch," a number of them were very holy, religious people. Although these gifts were deemed as "evil," they were never directly or indirectly used for that purpose.

If people possessed this gift in he stories of the Bible, why can't they possess it today? Again, it's the use of the gift that makes it good or evil.

It's all a matter of choice!

But what of the new generation? What choices will they make? What stories will they tell?

If I've learned two things throughout my life they are as follows:

- What comes around truly does go around.

- And, that one must learn to see with their soul and not their eyes, for eyes are controlled by the mind. Our human society mandates that our minds only accept logical explanations. Therefore, it will not allow thought or validation to what it considers to be illogical or non-tangible.

Don't ever think that chosen people aren't given special powers desired by both good and evil forces. For those who do not believe are marked as prey, easy to manipulate and ultimately own.

If one is to ever understand the worlds beyond this one, one must be receptive to the possibilities. It is only then that true sight and life's purpose will be achieved.

1

Early Exposure to the "World Beyond"

"May you squeal like a pig on your death bed!" This curse was cast upon a man in Portugal who had supposedly stolen my distant uncle's wife. And yes, that man did uncontrollably squeal like a pig on his deathbed!

There was also a story of a woman who apparently turned into a fly at night and tormented the local townspeople by buzzing and landing on them and their homes. The next day, she would be able to provide an account of what transpired in each home visited. When people confronted her regarding the private, personal knowledge she possessed, she would simply stare for a moment, smile and walk away.

These are only a few of my mother's many stories about our Portuguese ancestors.

Yeah, I know, maybe it was the power of suggestion or possibly some type of subliminal message that caused this man to squeal like a pig or the people to think this woman could change into the form of a fly. I thought so too until the unraveling of my life that has unfolded over the past forty-four years!

My mother's side of the family had numerous confrontations with both the "evil" and "good" sides of the spiritual word. Well, let's say, out of the ordinary experiences. Supposedly, as far back as the early 1800s, the townspeople had burned a number of my Portuguese descendants after trying and convicting them as witches.

I had always thought "witch burning" only occurred in Salem. However, my older aunts, great-grandparent and grandparents said that our relatives were unjustly burned simply because they possessed the unique ability to cure people afflicted with various illnesses, using special herbs.

One person, who possessed these special abilities, was actually given the name of "Witch Doctor." The ordinary townspeople didn't understand the usage of special herbs to cure people, which led to a massive panic and the burning of my relatives as witches.

Our Portuguese relatives also say that every generation has at least one or more child with "the gifts" described above. I found out later that both God and devil worshipers would be interested in "these unique gifts."

However, it didn't help to generate an understanding of our unique talents when curses, like the one of above, were used on people by my relatives. These acts definitely had the potential to give people the wrong impression. On a whole, I've found the Portuguese, including my relatives, to be both a very superstitious and fiercely religious people.

My mother's parents had migrated from Portugal to the states of New Hampshire and Rhode Island. Because Portuguese men were predominately fishermen by trade, Rhode Island and New Hampshire were perfect places to work and live.

As far back as I can remember, my relatives were extremely devout Catholics, which probably, indirectly, tied to the evil experienced throughout the generations. As my mother always said, "The more religious you are, the more the devil (evil) will antagonize you!" I have found this statement to be true!

I always wondered if my ancestral past was evil or if my relatives were simply provided with special gifts from God, such as the gift of healing and prophesy. The answer would be revealed later on in life.

However, this book does not focus on my relatives and their stories. This book focuses on my own experiences. My mother's sister also has a number of children with strange stories of their own. But I will save those stories for my next book. Let's begin: two brothers, Jack and Ted, and two sisters, Mary and Jane, and myself, Mosqeet, lived with my parents, Lorraine and Jack in a small, Rhode Island town.

Trust me, as a young child, I wondered the same thing. Why did my brothers and sisters have such commonly, ordinary names while I was given the name

"Mosqeet?" However, when I was about ten years old, my mother told me that great-grandmother, who shared the same name, asked that I be named Mosqeet.

My mother's great-grandmother had an illustrious past. Because she was able to cure critically ill people, she was accused of being a witch in Portugal. The local townspeople were in the process of gathering their evidence and plotting their strategy against her when she fled the country in order to avoid persecution. In Portugal, they were still torturing witches in the mid to late 1800s. It took only minimal evidence to convict someone of being a witch.

My mother's great-grandparents originally settled in Rhode Island. Unfortunately, with so many Portuguese people migrating to the North America, particularly the East Coast, my great-grandmother ran into the same problems with other Portuguese people who believed she was a witch or who recognized her from "the old country."

Although I believed my own great-grandmother when she told me that her mother was not a witch, I found the stories regarding her trips to Fall River, Massachusetts, bizarre. Basically, the purpose of these trips was to visit what she called a "religious healer." If my mother's great-grandmother had a need to either cure a sick relative or communicate with a dead relative, she would work with this person. This woman was called a "religious healer" because any spiritual interactions were performed in the name of God.

I didn't have too many details as to what transpired during those encounters. However, I do know that they involved burying religious statues, making them bleed, and cry, mixing herbs and intermingling the healer and seeker's blood. I truly believe that my mother's great-grandmother did believe this "religious healer's" powers were bestowed by God. However, since it just wasn't the type of behavior expected or accepted by "normal" society, my mother's great-grandmother was forced to flee once again.

To ensure her family's safety, my great-grandmother quickly moved them to New Hampshire, which was quite desolate during that time. However, a few years later, my mother's great-grandmother's son and daughter both move back to the state of Rhode Island.

As I reflected over the years on why I was named Mosqeet, I wondered if I was innocently given the name as a symbol of love for my great-great grandmother or if my mother had received some type of revelation that I would possess the abilities of my great, great-grandmother? Ironically, not only did I possess my great, great-grandmother's unique abilities but also both her physical appearance and intellectual characteristics. She was also thin and tall (5'5" is considered a giant's height to the Portuguese culture, during that period of time, whose people average five feet in height, especially the women) with large, oval, hazel eyes.

Although, my mother's heritage is Portuguese, my father's is not. He is mostly Irish and Scottish. However, my father became all too familiar with stories about my Portuguese relatives regarding superstitions and religious accounts.

As a child, my family and I lived in a run-down, rented house on the barroom part of town. My mother did everything she could to ensure that her children were safe, happy, provided for with life's necessities and loved. By her own fault, as some of us have also experienced, she blindly loved a man that wasn't right for her or her children.

My father was a self-absorbed man who thought of himself as being incredibly handsome, charming and a gift to the ladies. Needless to say, his time was only spent on himself. If my father wasn't at a bar or the dog track, he was usually with a variety of women. My father never demonstrated any visible expression of true love to either his wife or his children. But this only contributed to the special bond that my brothers, sisters and myself developed amongst ourselves and our mother.

So in this worn house, my first realization that there was an existence beyond this world we call reality came at about the age of four. Although this first spiritual encounter didn't directly happen to me, I was awakened by the yelling. Jack, who was about five years old, came running out of the bathroom begging me to go with him to see his twin. This scared me a little bit, specifically because Jack was not a twin. Unfortunately, by the time I got there, Jack's supposed twin was gone. Jack said that when he got up to go to the bathroom, his twin was in there waiting for him. The twin looked at him, laughed, vaporized and disappeared down the tub drain. For awhile, I believed he was dreaming, but this happened to him repeatedly throughout his childhood. Jack not only clearly saw himself but other people. Later on, during his adulthood years, different dead people routinely appeared and conversed with him, especially my grandmother.

Not too long after Jack's "bathroom" experience, my own personal experiences would follow. At the age of four, I developed a bad case of pneumonia in both lungs. The doctor said it was because I had been sleeping on a musty, moldy mattress that had been given to my mother. Unfortunately, only a day after being diagnosed, my oxygen intake had rapidly diminished and the rescue squad was called. While the rescue squad was on route to the hospital, I was put on oxygen and rushed immediately into the Emergency room. I ended up in a coma for several days.

On numerous occasions, during those comatose days, I would see myself in a small, weather-beaten, paint-peeled rowboat, floating down a jet-black river. Running along the muddy banks was a figure approximately six feet tall. This figure seemed to be made up of no substance, just numerous black-cloud mist pockets.

The Black-Cloud Mist Man (the name I have given to this apparition), besides being made up of mist, had a number of large, jagged, see-through holes. As my boat continued floating, the Black-Cloud Mist Man feverishly ran along the outer banks, trying to catch-up with me. Within the black mist, what appeared to be a head with misshapen eyes kept careful watch. But no matter how long I floated or how fast, the Black Cloud Mist Man could never catch up to me.

You don't have to remind me that I was a child with fever and in a coma, and that I was bound to have crazy dreams. For many years, I considered this incident as an experience common to that of an extremely sick child. However, that theory changed when later in my life, the Black Cloud Mist Man resurfaced while I was fully awake and in a healthy state.

Obviously, I did recover and eventually went home with no other peculiar incidents, until we moved to our new home. Well, actually, it was my grandparents' home. I didn't really know my father's family, but I did know my mother's parents, who were very loving, kind and, as mentioned earlier, religious people. When my grandparents met, they didn't realize they were related.

My grandfather was the child of my great, great-grandmother, who migrated from New Hampshire to Rhode Island. My grandmother was the daughter of my grandfather's sister, who also migrated from New Hampshire to Rhode Island. Did I lose any of you? In simpler terms, my grandfather was actually my grandmother's (his sister's daughter) uncle.

Although they didn't initially realize they were related, even after they did, they were already deeply in love and still wanted desperately to marry. In those days, as it is today, it was against the law to marry a relative in this country, so my grandparents went to Canada and got married.

I always compared my grandparents' situation with that of royalty. Yes, royalty. It is a known fact that long before the Renaissance period, royalty usually married relatives in an effort to keep the bloodlines pure. Unfortunately, what they didn't realize is their joining would actually have an adverse affect on their children. For like those kings and queens, my grandparents had several children that died as infants and toddlers, as well as two grown sons that died of diseases connected with their parents being related. I often wondered if this was caused by the intermingling of the same bloodline or if it was it the result of an old curse that had been supposedly placed on the family back in Portugal. Or, was it a punishment by God for forming a union that society deemed to be both illegal and immoral. Although my grandparents experienced a number of hardships, their love held strong and steady through each trial and tribulation endured.

Eventually, my grandparents saved enough money to purchase their own home when my mother was about five years old. The house was said to have previously been a pizza parlor, a dance hall and a secret prostitute hangout.

Supposedly, the original structure had accidentally been burned down, killing the prostitutes and "guests" inside. Needless to say, my grandfather required little money to purchase the house's remaining burnt shell. It was my grandfather's sweat that rebuilt that house into a home. My grandparents also turned the land into a small farm, which included some crops and a few animals. Although their house was old, years later it would be evident that my grandparents were consistent with its upkeep and maintenance.

Growing up, my mother and her family lived on this secluded farm. My mother would walk at least a mile to get to a main street or the nearest neighbor. Giant cornfields engulfed the land between the main road and my mother's home. One autumn night, my mother, a teenager at that time, took a short cut home through the dried, frost-kissed cornfields. Unexpectedly, she encountered people dressed in black clothing, repetitiously chanting and moving around a blazing fire. Although my mother saw them, they never did see her. The next day, when my mother went back to the site, the only remaining item was a symbol of devilworship burnt into the grass. After hearing this story, several questions came to my mind. Why was that particular spot chosen so close to my grandparents' home? There was at least a solid mile of consecutive rows and rows of cornfields and seclusion. Was it a coincidence or some type of unspoken connection?

As a small child, I remember spending a lot of happy times sitting among my grandparents' ever-blooming flowers, racing though the endless wide open fields and swinging and singing made-up songs on the tree-rope swing that my grandfather constructed. It was certainly a wonderful haven for me. I had always felt so safe and secure. It was all to end too soon. Sorrowfully, my grandfather died when I was six years old. With my grandmother's love of her life taken, she could no longer bear to stay in the house. Eventually, my grandmother would move to my aunt's house in North Carolina.

After my grandmother left, my family ended up moving into my grandparents' house. My father liked it. It was rent-free! By 1965, a number of houses had sprung up around my grandparents' house. Actual streets began forming and entire neighborhoods took shape. It wasn't too long before my grandparents' once beautifully, well-kept house had become dilapidated and broken-down. Unfortunately, my father didn't love the home like my grandfather and was not repair-savvy or conscientious.

The neighborhood kids really taunted us, especially at Halloween. Our house was voted most likely to be haunted. They didn't realize that there was actually some truth to their teasing, for during this time, bizarre occurrences had already taken place.

I remember the very first incident that occurred after first moving into the house. My father came running out of my parents' bedroom screaming after coming home late one night. Apparently, my father had gotten into a fight with my mother and when he tried to hit her, he swears, to this day, that my mother's statue of St. Anthony jumped off her bureau, transformed into a life-sized version and tried to attack him. My mother had always had a special devotion and love for St. Anthony, something that my unreligious father would not understand. I truly believe that St. Anthony came to my mother's aid that night.

But my greatest memories of the house were of the infamous upstairs attic. One particular night, when I was about eight, I heard someone, in a low, gruff, slow, deep voice calling the name "Lorraine, Lorraine" over and over. As I left my room and followed the voice into my brothers' room, which was unoccupied at the time, the voice became both clear and familiar. It sounded like my grandfather (who, as you know, had died several years earlier). From my brothers' room, I approached the steps that led to the attic. The voice was now crystal clear. It was my grandfather, and he was calling for his daughter, my mother. As I tried cautiously walking up those creaky, old attic stairs, making as little noise as possible, the voice suddenly stopped. It was almost as if my grandfather had decided to silently await my arrival. Because there were no handrails I had to use the wall to guide my way. I could feel the edges of the crinkled, stiff flower wallpaper that had been partially torn from the walls from being so aged. After walking up approximately three steps, I became too frightened to go on. And with my heart wildly pounding, I turned around, ran down the stairs, out of my brothers' room, into the dark, unlit hall, into my room and under the secure covers of my bed.

Why was my grandfather calling my mother? Was it a call for help? Was it a longing call in hopes to see her again? Was it a warning call that would foretell of her future life's misery? And why did my grandfather stop calling when he knew I was approaching? Did he assume I was my mother? My grandfather's mournful call was heard again by some of the other kids but oddly, never by my mother.

Ironically, after the house was eventually sold, my aunt, who lived nearby, told us that the couple who bought the house asked if someone by the name of "Lorraine" had lived in it. Without divulging any information, my aunt asked why. With hesitation, fearful they would be thought of as crazy, they told my aunt that on numerous occasions they could hear a man's voice calling for a "Lorraine." My aunt had never been told of the stories of how the children heard my grandfather calling for our mother.

For most of our time spent at the house, constant voices and footsteps pacing back and forth could be heard in the attic. However, when anyone ever approached the stairs, they would immediately stop. I always wondered why spirits had felt the need to hide in the attic. Were they banished to the attic? Were they not allowed to stay among the people they once knew? Was this some type of punishment, or did they simply choose not to walk among the evil that consumed so much of humanity.

Regardless of the strange occurrences that transpired, my childhood while living at my grandparents' house was filled with wonderful memories. Well, with one exception—our neighbor, who I will affectionately called "Fatso DaSilva."

Fatso DaSilva was a woman who had come from the same vicinity of Portugal as my great-grandmother and her children. Therefore, my grandparents knew her well, and of her truly evil reputation. It was meeting and getting to know this woman that helped me understand the distinction between people who used their special gifts/powers for evil verses those who used them for good. My family was given special gifts to cure people, prophesize, and have out-of-body experiences; I believed that they were "God-given abilities." However, I am convinced that people like "Fatso DaSilva" got their abilities from dark, unholy forces.

Every neighborhood has its Fatso DaSilva but she different. Yes, she was your run-of-the-mill "mean neighborhood lady," always yelling at the kids, chasing them away if they were remotely near her yard, keeping accidentally thrown baseballs and spying into close neighbors' homes with her binoculars. But there was something different about Fatso DaSilva. There was more to her than just being mean.

Fatso DaSilva looked just like her name. She was about five feet tall and five feet wide. She had ink-black hair that was teased into a beehive style. Fatso DaSilva also had black, cat-eye shaped eyeglasses, non-distinct eyes, tiny, almost invisible lips and a distinct Portuguese/American accent.

Let's not forget her dog, "Princess," or should I say, her "familiar." For those of you who do not recognize the term "familiar," it means an animal that carry out the commands of its witch master. Princess sure fit that description.

Princess was a sandy-colored Chihuahua. Often, Princess could be seen mysteriously slinking around, carrying personal objects of the neighborhood kids over to the waiting hands of Fatso DaSilva. Once obtained by Fatso DaSilva, these objects would never be seen again but were definitely used.

I'm sure you're wondering how these objections were used? I believe that Fatso DaSilva used each kid's personal object to inflict some kind of emotional or physical pain, similar to how objects are used when practicing voodoo.

And like most familiars, Princess was horrified of Fatso DaSilva. Anytime Princess encountered Fatso DaSilva, her ears would sink down to the ground and her tail would disappear almost completely beneath her body. But Princess always followed her directions. Although Princess was carrying out the evil bidding of her master, I still felt sorry for the dog. Princess was just another pawn in this web of evil, as was Fatso DaSilva's son, Maurice.

Maurice was quite the opposite. He was meek and rather nerdy-looking. Maurice was never allowed to leave his house or play with any kids. As a matter of fact, I'm not even sure if he ever went to school. Maurice was never on the school bus, nor was he ever seen in any of the various schools in town. The only glimpses we had of Fatso DaSilva's son were through his bedroom window. Sometimes, we would catch Maurice longingly watching us play. Even though Maurice was Fatso DaSilva's son, I didn't get an evil vibe from his stares. They were more sorrowful and pitiful in nature. I'm sure Fatso DaSilva never allowed Maurice to go outside or play with the neighborhood kids for fear her identity would be exposed.

However, most of Fatso DaSilva's evil deeds were conducted in an unspoken manner. If Fatso DaSilva happened to be staring out her from parlor window, sitting on her front porch or standing in her yard and one of the kids happened to be riding by on their bike, running or just sitting on the neighborhood "Big Rock," (a large boulder that sat in a neighbor's yard) that kid would literally be struck in their tracks. When it first happened to me, I thought it was just an accident. But when my unexplained accidents kept reoccurring, I started to observe the pattern. Then it happened! After falling from my bike, my eyes just happened to immediately fix themselves onto Fatso DaSilva's house. As Fatso DaSilva sat on her front porch, her knifelike piercing eyes attached themselves to mine. With that, she slowly smiled, got up from her bench and went into the house. To her satisfaction, it was almost as if she was saying, "My work here is done" without uttering a word.

However, two could play at that game, and I didn't need personal objects to do it. I had found that, as a child, if I wished vengefully for something bad to happen to someone or something, it would. At that time, I didn't realize how dangerous being vengeful could be. I was predisposing myself to future evil. Needless to say, in situations where I am extremely angry, it is very difficult to diffuse these feelings. Sometimes I'm afraid I'll uncontrollably allow myself to act upon those feelings, later regretting the outcome. But at that time, I decided that Fatso DaSilva would be the object of my revenge.

It wasn't going to be anything elaborate or life threatening. I simply desired that Fatso DaSilva would experience some of the physical pain us neighborhood kids had felt at her hands. It might have been a coincidence, but a neighborhood car wreck and a broken pelvis later, Fatso DaSilva was confined to her bed.

Although I'm digressing a little, this reminds me of a similar incident I experienced in the second grade. My obese, large-headed teacher used to taunt me because I was so paper-thin. For example, on a daily basis, she would intentionally drop a pencil behind the bookcase that sat inches away from the wall. She would then have the class stop what they were doing to watch me go and retrieve the pencil. Once retrieved, she would make one of her infamous derogatory statements, such as, "See the walking toothpick, look at the scarecrow," and start laughing along with the class.

One day, as I sat with my class in our classroom eating lunch, I watched my teacher carefully peeling off the green and brown parts of her greasy potato chip and proceeded to shove them one by one into her mouth. Because of her constant taunting I despised her, and on that particular day, an intense feeling came over me. I started to wish she would have an accident, leaving her unable to teach for the rest of the year. As my eyes stayed fixed on this cruel teacher, her solid, brown-stained, oak chair broke apart into a million pieces, and with a look of horror on her face, she fell and went crashing to the ground. I don't remember all the specific details, but I do remember the rescue squad taking her away. I later learned that she had broken her back. The principal ended up taking her place for the rest of the year. Needless to say, I was happy that she would be unable to taunt me for the rest of the year. I did see her later in life, looking haggard and walking with a slight limp. The feelings I had that day were the same feelings I experienced when Fatso DaSilva had her unfortunate accident.

Anyway, let's get back to Fatso DaSilva. Since her bedroom faced the front part of the house, she was able to pull up her blinds and look out the window, continuing her reign of terror. And unfortunately, Fatso DaSilva knew whom to thank for her incarceration. I would soon discover that her wrath would not be directed at me, but someone close to me.

Shortly after her unfortunate accident, I recall several neighbor kids running into our house with my youngest sister, Jane. Jane had just fallen off the Big Rock. Jane told us that while she was playing at the top of the Big Rock, she had felt a weird sensation. It was as if someone or something were standing over her. When Jane looked up from the Big Rock, she saw Fatso DaSilva peering through her blinds. As she slowly shut them, Jane fell. Was this a coincidence? Could Jane's fall be attributed to past stories regarding Fatso DaSilva's unusual "powers" observed while in Portugal? Or had Jane simply imagined the incident after hearing the kids talk about our neighborhood witch, Fatso DaSilva.

Well, no, it couldn't possibly be the last scenario. The kids in the neighborhood didn't hang around with Jane because she was six years younger than we were. So Jane never got to hear any of the Fatso DaSilva stories. Also, it wasn't until Jane's fall that the neighborhood kids got together and started talking about similar falling experiences under the watchful eye of Fatso DaSilva or, as my mother would say, "The evil eye" of Fatso DaSilva. I guess Fatso DaSilva had gotten her revenge, or so I thought. Although her pattern was realized, the torment didn't end.

The worst incident of all was about to happen to Jane. Jane was maybe one or two years older than when she had experienced the previous incident. Jane was riding her bike and crashed violently into, of all places, Fatso DaSilva's tree. For weeks, besides all the bumps, bruises and right leg limp, Jane had lost some of her memory and her speech was impaired. Jack, who had witnessed the crash, noticed that Fatso DaSilva was watering her grass when her eyes looked up and immediately locked on Jane. When Jane crashed, instead of showing concern and offering her assistance, Fatso DaSilva immediately went into her house and shut all the blinds.

One to two years after Fatso DaSilva's accident, I would come to learn that curses didn't necessarily happen instantaneously. They could be inflicted when you least expected them. Circumstantial timing had to be perfect. Elaborate, complicated curses might take years to unfold. But whether the results of the curse were immediate or futuristic, the results were the same; they were devastating.

Now, maybe those incidents still don't seem like much to you, but the ultimate test was to soon reveal the truth. One day, Fatso DaSilva was engaged in a verbal confrontation, over her fence, with my mother. As Fatso DaSilva got out of her house and stomped into our yard, she suddenly stopped dead in her tracks. She seemed almost like a vampire suddenly realizing that the sun was rising, or when trying to bite his victim, noticing that a cross or string of garlic was being worn. For some reason, Fatso DaSilva could not proceed toward our front steps. She then proceeded to ask my mother why her broom was turned upside down. My mother replied, "You know why, you **Feiteceia**!" Apparently, when my mother was done sweeping our front steps, she would always turn the broom upside down. To this day, the superstitious Portuguese believe that a witch cannot enter someone's house when a broom was turned upside down at the entrance. Therefore, Fatso DaSilva could not advance any closer to our house. That was when the truth was revealed. For Fatso DaSilva was aware that we were now able to confirm why she could no longer proceed. In essence, this truth would render her powerless against my family. But it was no surprise to me, for I had known her true identify all along. Fatso DaSilva's reign of terror was coming to an end. Fatso DaSilva, Maurice and Princess quickly and quietly moved from the neighborhood.

Even though Fatso DaSilva wreaked havoc throughout my childhood years, I did have one both extraordinary and positive experience during that time. Sorrowfully, the mother of my best friend, Sharon Hanson, died in childbirth as well as her baby. She left her husband and four other children behind. Sharon was about twelve years old. Sharon's mother also happened to be my mother's best friend. After her death, my mother provided day care for both the two- and one-year-old babies while Sharon's father went to work at night. Unfortunately, that left Sharon responsible for watching her younger sister. After supper, I use to go over at night to keep Sharon company.

One night, Sharon had to stay at school late to work on a project, so I was asked to baby-sit. As Sharon's younger sister played in the living room and I watched television, I started to hear a low hum from down the hall. Sharon lived in a one-story ranch with what seemed to be a never-ending hall. As I got up from the couch and started to walk down the hall, the humming turned into singing. I didn't recognize the song. Actually, I didn't recognize the language. I seemed to be the only one aware of the singing, because as I looked over at Sharon's sister, hoping she would also acknowledge the singing, she just continued happily playing.

I gathered up my courage and continued to walk down the hall. The music was coming from Sharon's father's bedroom. As I carefully approached the door, the singing continued. As I pressed myself against the wall and peeked around the corner, I immediately froze as the adrenaline coursed through every part of my body. There was Sharon's dead mother, joyfully and peacefully rocking back and forth in the rocking chair, which had been so carefully safeguarded, with her dead baby tenderly cradled in her arms. She never acknowledged my presence and never looked up. She just continued to rock. It was as if she and I were simultaneously living in two different dimensions. Somehow, managing to move my lead-balloon legs, I ran back to the living room, grabbed Sharon's confused sister and ran across the rock-covered road into my house.

I didn't know why I was so frightened. Sharon's mother was a wonderful woman. The apparition that I saw wasn't scary or ugly. I think it was just the fear of seeing something that you know shouldn't exist. Notice that I used the words "shouldn't exist" and not "doesn't exist." I believed Sharon's mother was in that rocking chair. The only person I ever told this story to was my mother. And of course, she knew all too well that it was entirely possible. Although I never saw Sharon's mother again, from time to time, I did hear a low, sweet hum coming from that room and the faint squeak of a rocking chair.

As you can see, for the most part, I lived the life of your average pre-teen. The real excitement started when I was in my early teens. Specifically, when I was told I was a witch.

2

Me, a Witch?

As my childhood quickly turned into my early teen years, my supernatural experiences were just beginning. By the time I was thirteen, my life had taken quite a turn. At this age, I had my first real boyfriend, Zach Colt. It occurred to me that his last name was probably fabricated. For Zach's family had also smuggled themselves from Portugal, and in doing so, changed their last name. I never really found out why they were forced to smuggle themselves into this country instead of arriving legitimately.

Zach was my first real love. He was blessed with a perfect olive-colored skin tone, a matching shade of soft, brown eyes and naturally loose, curly hair that just draped over the back of his neck. Even today, I can still visualize those white teeth, perfectly structured with the exception of the slight chip in his left tooth.

Zach's only downfall, so I thought, was his age. Zach was four years older than me. That's a lot when you're only thirteen! But being thirteen back in the seventies was equivalent to being at least sixteen, if not older, today. We were much more mature then, which wasn't necessarily a good thing.

Zach also had the coolest car! It was a '71 white Pinto with a black pin stripe on both sides of the car, and four oversized tires. At thirteen years of age, I felt like the epitome of cool riding around in that souped up Pinto. Zach worked as a mechanic in a local garage. However, for fun, Zach raced sponsored cars at a local speedway. Every Saturday I would be at that racetrack cheering him on.

At that time, my life couldn't have been more perfect! I was in love for the first time and all was right with the world. But those euphoric feelings were suddenly overshadowed by feelings of unhappiness and sorrow. My mother had just confirmed what she had suspected all along. My father was having an affair with yet another woman, a teenager that was only five years older than I was! Unfortunately, my mother was able to prove her suspicions this time.

Needless to say, my mother plunged into the depths of despair and helplessness. She would start her day off crying and end it crying. Even though my mother had five children, she seemed lost and alone. Feeling that my mother needed to get away from this depressing situation and spend time with people that really loved her, my grandmother sent bus fare for all of us to come and visit with her in North Carolina.

I hated leaving Zach, but my mother's welfare was much more important to me. It was imperative that we tried to rebuild ourselves into this new family structure. So, one early July morning, my mother, two brothers, two sisters, and I boarded a bus bound for North Carolina.

As you may recall earlier in the story, after my grandfather died, my grandmother moved to North Carolina to live with my aunt and uncle. Their home was located in a picturesque town located near the top of the Smokey Mountains.

Even though the trip would be long, I was looking forward to seeing my grandmother, Aunt Elsie, Uncle Bill and my ten cousins. Fortunately, I had also mentally prepared myself for this close to twenty-six hour journey we were about to embark upon. However, I wasn't prepared for what transpired shortly after! Now, I don't know if you've ever taken a bus ride to a faraway destination, but if you ever do, prepare yourself to stop frequently along the way.

I believe that my bizarre encounter occurred somewhere after the bus stopped in New York. My mother, who was fearful that we might be subjected to undesirables if we departed from the bus, insisted that we stay on board. My brother Jack was approximately three rows behind the bus driver on the right-hand side. Jack, who was already fourteen, was at that age where he didn't want to be seen with his family, so he sat alone, leaning up against the window. My sister Mary and brother Ted sat in two seats together on the left-hand side of the bus, approximately five rows from the bus driver. Now, I was sitting probably halfway down the bus, on the left-hand side, near the window, also alone. My sister Jane, being the youngest, got to sit with my mother on the right hand side of the bus, in the very last row.

As we sat on the bus in that dark bus depot, waiting for the additional passengers to come aboard, I couldn't help but wonder what Zach was doing. I was already missing him. But my thoughts of Zach quickly refocused to the scuffling feet of the people who were starting to board the bus. As I watched people enter, I started daydreaming about their lives, why they were on the bus, where were they going, why weren't they flying like smart people do!

Almost startled, I noticed a middle-aged woman. She was about 5'7" and slightly overweight, with what appeared to be excessively black dyed hair. The woman, who was dressed in a plain black, polyester and nylon dress, also wore a black laced veil, which was draped around her head but not over her face. She also wore a long black poncho-styled outer garment, a large chain with several hanging, symbol medallions, numerous antique styled rings and bold make-up and nail polish. This woman stopped at Jack's row and slithered herself into the seat next to him.

Quite frankly, I didn't give it another thought! I quickly turned back to reading my romance novel and devouring the penny candies I had brought with me. I thought how lucky I was that no one had occupied the empty seat next to me! From time to time, I would notice Jack conversing with this woman. However, I was too busy either reading or ensuring that Mary and Ted were still in their seats.

After several hours passed, Jack came back to where I was sitting. He plopped into the seat next to me. The look on his face was that of total astonishment. Then, Jack said something to me that I've never forgotten to this day. Jack told me that the woman sitting near him said that she was a witch. The woman told Jack that she belonged to a "cult" that was based in New York City. The woman told Jack that the only reason she was on the bus was to "talk to you." Puzzled, I said to Jack, "What does that woman want to talk to you about?" Agitated, Jack said, "No, she wants to talk to YOU." Immediately, I thought that Jack was trying to scare me, as any normal big brother loved doing. But I had never seen Jack so intense. His watery, grey-blue eyes were wild with excitement and wonder. Jack was noticeably hyperventilating with each word he spoke. He was in awe with this woman's ability to point out his brother and sisters on this crowded bus, especially since we were all scattered. What was even more amazing was that the woman knew very specific things about me.

Out of all my brothers and sisters, she only referenced personal facts about Jack and me. She knew my full name, date of birth, my likes, dislikes, and could provide information regarding past and current events. This woman also knew all about Zach and described specific details of our relationship, such as how we met, Zach's after-school job, and the fact he raced cars. It was frighteningly incredible!

Apparently, this woman told Jack that she was sent by her "cult" to talk to me about joining them. The cult felt that I had special "talents" that would be beneficial to them. She said that if I joined them, I would be made part of the cult's governing force. She told Jack that I already had the ability to prophesize and engage in out-of-body transportation. She also said that I had other "talents" that they could help me to develop.

However, the woman also stated that there was one potential problem. It was with my religious beliefs. She alluded to the fact that because of my religious convictions, I could be just as powerful in my church as I could be in her cult. This woman knew that I was a firm believer in God and would eventually witness his powerful works (which, by the way, are also described in this book). Although I went to church every Sunday and believed in its teachings, I didn't see myself as an overly religious thirteen-year-old. But this woman's statement would prove to be factual in the future.

Now, she also told Jack that the reason she came to him was that he and I both possessed these special talents. However, she said that Jack had the ability to only "receive" information, such as spirit visitations, but that he was not able to "provide" information, i.e., communicating with the dead or out-of-body transportation. Therefore, Jack was of no particular interest to her and the cult.

However, this woman asked Jack if he could somehow convince me to sit with her on the bus to discuss the possibilities. As Jack continued talking, I became increasingly apprehensive and confused. How did this woman know me? What did this cult want from me? Why was this woman telling my brother that I was a witch? Did this mean that I was really evil, or had the potential of becoming evil? And as foretold by past generations of my ancestors, was I to be this generation's Feiteceira (Portuguese Witch)?

I noticed this woman was now completely turned around in her seat, intently watching me and eagerly waiting for signs regarding my response. I'm sure my response was not what she had expected. I told Jack that I wasn't interested and didn't want that woman anywhere near me. I also immediately retreated to the back of the bus and informed my mother what was happening at the front of the bus. I also told her what that witch was saying about me. My mother calmly told me to remain in the back of the bus and try ignoring her.

Oddly, my mother didn't try to comfort me with reassuring words, such as "The woman is disturbed" or "She is just trying to scare you" or even "Jack just made up the story." The frightening thing of it all was that I knew my mother believed this woman was really a witch. I couldn't help but wonder why my mother was so accepting of this woman's proclamation. Did she know something I didn't?

However, my mother immediately called Jack and the other kids to the back of the bus. Jack, who had returned back to his seat with the disappointing news, tried to persuade the woman into coming to the back of the bus and providing my mother with her detailed information and purpose. Jack was totally fascinated with this woman. He would have surely been an easy mark, if they wanted him! But the woman immediately declined. She told my brother that she couldn't go anywhere near the back of the bus because she knew my mother was praying.

You see, my mother knew that this witch could not come to the back of the bus as long as she continued to pray. So, with a strong conviction and show of religious power, my mother proudly displayed her rosary beads in full sight. For you non-Catholics, rosary beads are used to recite prayers to glorify and honor Jesus' mother, Our Blessed Mother Mary. With that, the witch simply turned around, faced forward and remained in her seat for the rest of the night, or at least I thought did.

Now the bus we were on was non-stop to North Carolina. We were told that the bus would not be making any additional stops for gas or other passengers. It was approaching nine or ten o'clock and the passengers began to settle in for the long night's ride ahead. Even after all that excitement, somehow, my family all managed to fall asleep.

However, about six o'clock that morning, I was the first to wake up. As I looked around, I noticed Jane with her head on my mother's lap. Jack, Ted and Mary all had their mouths opened, asleep in their seats. Suddenly, I remembered, the witch. However, from the back row of the bus, as I looked for her in the designated row, she was nowhere to be found. So with my eyes quickly scanning, I began thoroughly searching the right side of the bus and then the left. Still, she was no where to be found! I quietly got up from my seat and started walking up and down the rows to find her, but she was gone. I waited to see if she would come out of the bathroom, but she never did.

Almost in a panic, I went to the front of the bus to ask the bus driver if he had made any stops during the night. The bus driver said no stops were made and sharply reminded me that this was a non-stop trip. Even so, I foolishly asked the bus driver again if he was sure no stops had been made during the night, which, by the way, you should never do after someone's been driving non-stop for eight or more hours.

Anyway, she was gone! But how could this be? I know I didn't imagine this whole thing, or did I? Just then, Jack came running up the aisle of the bus. The first question out of his mouth was, "Where's the witch?" Well, at least that confirmed I wasn't dreaming! Jack and I returned to the back of the bus to my mother. Surprisingly, my mother didn't seem shocked. She acted as if this whole occurrence was nothing out of the ordinary.

As Jack and I tried to make sense of it all, my mother, in a slow, calm voice said, "She's gone, so let's forget about it."

Several hours later, the bus finally stopped in North Carolina. It felt so good to be able to stretch our legs and touch the ground again. But most importantly, this rest stop had a real bathroom. We approached the men's room and my brothers went in. We had to walk a little way to the ladies' room. As usual, an extensive line had formed leading into the ladies' room. Finally, as we approached the opening of the door, we noticed that leaning up against the back wall of the ladies' room was the witch from the bus.

At first, the witch tried taking a few steps toward us, but immediately froze in her tracks. I realized that she couldn't get close to me; my mother was still holding on to her rosary beads for dear life. In a weird way, those rosary beads were almost like my mother holding onto a gun or some other type of weapon. Without saying a word, my mother quickly moved us back to the men's room door, picked up my brothers and headed to another ladies' room in the building. Even though she didn't say it, my mother must have been frightened, because she forced the boys to go into the ladies' room and wait for us.

After leaving the ladies' room, we were immediately whisked back to the bus. As we were walking back on the bus, Jack shouted, "There she is!" As I turned to see what he was shouting about, the self-proclaimed witch was standing off to the left-hand side of the bus, her eyes fixed on me as she silently waited and watched.

The witch finally spoke directly to me. She simply stated, "Bye for now, Mosqeet. Be assured that we will meet later." The woman didn't actually disappear—she literally faded into an unobservant crowd.

As we were reseated on the bus, a million questions began surfacing in my mind. First, how did this woman get off the bus when it never stopped during the night? Second, how did she know that we were going to go to this specific bathroom? There were at least ten ladies' rooms in this large terminal. Third, what did she want from me? And finally, why was I so important to her? As I sat there a few minutes agonizing over these questions and formulating possible answers, Jack came and sat beside me.

Jack told me that the witch was also at the men's room door. The witch told Jack that she would return and that she and I would have a future encounter. She explained that it might not necessarily be in the form that she was currently appearing in, but that we would officially meet and it wouldn't be under such pleasant circumstances. Other methods of persuasion were now necessary because of my unwillingness to speak to her or accept her invitation. Although her statement initially frightened me, I was more intrigued with how she could be at the men's room and the ladies' room at the same time. There was obviously so much I didn't understand. Thank God the remainder of the trip to our North Carolina destination, as well as the trip home, was uneventful.

When I returned home, I didn't dare share my experience with Zach. I knew that he wouldn't understand. He probably would have thought I needed psychological help! However, with his Portuguese background, maybe he would have understood. I wasn't prepared to take that chance. I didn't talk about the incident to anyone.

After returning home, I spent weeks trying to sort out what had transpired. I tried desperately to reason out the entire incident. However, eventually, I had to give up. I knew that I needed to stop dwelling on this experience and go on living my life as normally as possible. However, I've never experienced what most people classified as an "ordinary" life.

Little did I realize the best was yet to come. Chapter Three will really describe the foundation of my supernatural experiences, so read on!

3

Werewolf, Scott and the Ouija Board

At the age of sixteen, my relationship with Zach, like most first loves, ended quite abruptly and without warning. Zach cheated on me with a girl that supposedly looked exactly like me. So needless to say, like every insecure young girl, I felt that there must have been something wrong with me. It couldn't have possibly been that Zach was just a loser! No actually, he was more warped, who gets involved with another girl who looks like the girl you just dumped! Everyone supposedly has someone who looks like them out in the world. Isn't it a strange coincidence that my "look-alike" happened to steal my boyfriend?

But over the passing years, I would eventually feel differently. Zach ended up cheating on his wife (the girl who looked like me) numerous times, and they ultimately ended up divorced. I am a firm believer in what comes around goes around. I've witnessed it so many times during my life. It's terrible to admit but I felt sheer satisfaction when I learned of Zach's misfortune. But, at the same time, I was also a little nervous that it might have been my fault. I had begun to realize that often, when I intently wished for something bad to happen to someone, it came to fruition!

Anyway, the break up with my first love was not an easy one, but I rebounded quickly. I started hanging out with my childhood friend Sharon. That usually meant trouble was ahead. Back in the seventies, it was a cool thing to hang around on the main street of your hometown. Living in the state of Rhode Island, my hometown was your typically pre-Revolutionary-War-structured New England town. Downtown, there were a number of historically preserved buildings, including early colonial-mansion-style homes, white marble schools, an old brick bakery, a hotel and other specialty shops constructed in the early 1700s.

Also, just one street over from the main street, a majestic harbor with continuously flowing waves could be seen no matter where you were standing. I remember studying in school about the important part this harbor played in the Revolutionary War. I didn't really appreciate the beauty of this town until many years later. Although downtown was extremely picturesque, it wasn't the sort of place you'd think teenagers would find exciting.

However, whenever possible, with my favorite name-embroidered shirt, which I had gotten from a gas-station-attendant friend, and my size three patched-up bell-bottoms, Sharon and I would take a walk downtown to check out the action. During that time, it was so important to be liked by one of the "downtown guys." Most of the guys who hung around downtown had cool nicknames and notorious reputations to match.

It was right around the Fourth of July when Sharon and I met "Werewolf." Sharon, Werewolf and I all happened to be standing in the same refreshment aisle at the town's carnival, held in our "common." (A New England town's common is located in the center of town. The first settlers use to take their animals to this centralized place for grazing purposes.)

I'm not sure where he got the name, because he sure didn't look like a "werewolf." Werewolf seemed unlike most of the guys we'd met downtown. Although apparently young, he seemed much more sophisticated and mature than the other guys we had encountered. Werewolf was really nothing special to look at and had no outstanding features. He had tiny brown eyes and a compact smile. He was short of stature with a bronze complexion. I assumed he was either Italian or Portuguese. If you lived in Rhode Island, usually your nationality was one or the other. Although there was nothing physically appealing about him, his voice was extremely mesmerizing. I could listen to him talk for hours. It made me feel so calm and relaxed, almost as if my life's spirit had detached itself from my body.

Over the next several weeks, Sharon and I would meet Werewolf in front of one of the downtown schools. Werewolf portrayed himself as a philosophical thinker. He came across as being "really deep." I found him to be most intriguing. On a cool, mid-August night, instead of sitting in front of our usual school, trying to analyze the world, Werewolf actually invited us to go to a party with him. I found this to be odd since we had never gone anywhere with Werewolf, even for a hamburger. However, the chance for Sharon and me to go to a party sounded appealing. This would be a great opportunity to meet other cool guys, like Werewolf.

We walked at least five blocks before arriving at a historically significant but weatherworn colonial mansion. As we walked inside, Werewolf quickly turned the lights on; to our surprise, the house had been converted into several apartments. After walking up a long, solid-oak stained staircase, Werewolf stopped at a door. It seemed as if time stood still as he slowly turned the handle. Suddenly, an unfounded feeling of apprehension consumed me.

When the door opened, all I could see was a crowded living room, filled with so many people that no one could move. As soon as I entered, it seemed as if everyone stopped talking and began staring at me. However, there was something else a little unusual about them—they were all nude! Both guys and girls were completely nude! Although only for a split second, I could see that in the middle of the room was a table draped with a discolored, wrinkled white tablecloth and one large burning red candle. Underneath the candle was the symbol that signified devil worship.

As Werewolf entered the apartment, all heads slightly bowed in adoration. Now aware of who and what Werewolf was, a wave of sheer panic came over me. Werewolf's tone of voice was much more mesmerizing than usual. Although he was asking us to come and join him and his friends—followers were more like it—I felt as if it was more of a "command" than a request. With that, I quickly grabbed Sharon's arm and we ran down those stairs as if our life depended upon it (if not our lives, our souls sure did). As we ran out of the building, we continued frantically running toward our neighborhood until our sides started to hurt.

It had been three years since "the bus" incident and I had almost forgotten what the witch had told me. She said that I would continue to be stalked throughout my life until I agreed to become part of them. Although Sharon and I tried to make light of the situation and chalked it up as a really bizarre but "cool experience," it was an all too real of a reminder for me. I would now have to be much more cautious. After that incident, Sharon and I never really did go back downtown to hang around. Instead, we started hanging around local ice cream stores and hamburger joints with our gas-station, car fanatic friends.

It was at the New England Creamery ice cream store that I had indirectly met another friend of Zach. Actually, it was someone who lived in the same neighborhood. His name was Scott Mendes. Like Zach, Scott was also older than I was, but by six years instead of four. Granted, I grew up in a small, Rhode Island town, but I also found meeting someone who grew up in Zach's neighborhood to be too coincidental. The town wasn't that small. Initially, Scott had presented himself in a quiet, soft-spoken manner. Scott had long, silky auburn hair and a mustache to match. Scott also happened to be part Portuguese, just like me.

Although Scott and I made "small talk" at the New England Creamery, no formal introductions were made. However, I ultimately did meet Scott through an arranged meeting that my younger brother, Ted, and Scott's brother had set-up. Our two brothers were best friends. After seeing me, Scott had secretly asked the boys to set up the introductory meeting. I never did understand how Scott knew that I was the sister of his little brother's friend. Our brothers were too little to hang around the places we hung out at. And supposedly, the New England Creamery was the first place that Scott had seen me. I know I sound overly suspicious—perhaps even borderline paranoid—but in light of the incidents that had transpired so far, I felt my feelings were justified.

Initially, I wasn't interested in Scott; I was still longing for Zach. But Scott cleverly enticed me with gossip about Zach and his new girlfriend. So I went out with him just to get the scoop. However, it didn't take me long to warm up to Scott. He had a certain alluring charm. In a matter of no time, I was introduced to his whole family. Scott had three sisters and two brothers. They really weren't anything out of the ordinary. However, his mother was a different story.

I'll never forget meeting Mrs. Mendes. The first thing I noticed about her was her striking, light, sky-blue eyes and mischievous curved-up lips. I didn't understand the word "aura" until I met her. When meeting her for the first time, a bizarre, uncomfortable feeling came over me. It was so odd. I'd never felt anything like it before. Mrs. Mendes was definitely different. What woman, or for that matter, mother whips open a "Playgirl" magazine to show her son's girlfriend the centerfold on their first encounter—or on any encounter, for that matter? Being raised in a religious family, it certainly wasn't behavior I was accustomed to. For some reason, she was always trying to get a reaction from me. But I wouldn't realize how different Mrs. Mendes was until much later on.

Like mine, Scott's father was your ordinary drunk. A short, dark man, he was exactly what someone might think the stereotypical full-blooded Portuguese man would look like. However, I've met a number of blond or red-haired, blue-eyed, fully-blooded Portuguese before as well. Actually, my grandfather had red hair, pea-green eyes and white-as-milk skin, while my grandmother had more of an olive-colored completion, dark brown hair and small but delicate, loving brown eyes. It all depends upon what part of Portugal you or your ancestors came from.

Anyway, even after meeting the clan, Scott and I continued to date. Scott took me to all types of restaurants, miniature golf, bowling and other amusements. It was certainly a thrilling time for a girl my age. Even though I was so wrapped up in Scott, I didn't forget my friends. There was one particular day when I went over to visit my friends Sharon, Paul and Peter. They were intensely involved in maneuvering around the dreaded Ouija board on Sharon's front steps.

My mother had always warned me about playing with the Ouija board. She believed that evil spirits were able to control the board. But being like every other teenager that wanted to do exactly what their parents didn't want them to do, I sat down to play. And with my friend Sharon on the other side, I asked the Ouija board my first and only question.

"What will my husband's name be?" I was secretly hoping it would be Scott. As I laid my hands on the board, it started to move. My hands and fingers felt weightless. I knew I wasn't moving the board, but was my friend Sharon?

To no one's surprise, the Ouija board spelled out the name "Scott." I knew I didn't do it, and Sharon also swore she hadn't moved the board. So then I thought, "Could this board actually be controlled by the power of suggestion?" I did want it to be Scott so badly. Was I actually able to move the board with my mind?

But then something strange happened. With my hands and Sharon's hands still on the Ouija board, it started to move again. This time, it spelled out the name, "WAYNE." Now, the only Wayne I knew was Scott's one-year-younger brother, who, I knew was also interested in me. Was something going to happen between Scott and me? Was I going to eventually end up with Scott's brother Wayne?

As you read on, pay close attention. The answer will be revealed.

Scott was renting a small house within a very Portuguese neighborhood. This made it very easy for us to be alone. It was nice to be able to get away, even if only for a little while, from the confusion of everything going on at home.

During the early course of our relationship, I had found out that Scott had been briefly married for about ten months. Scott and his wife had divorced about three months prior to our first meeting. Apparently, Scott had gone out with Elizabeth for several years before they got married. But most of that time was spent waiting for Scott to come home from Vietnam. Once they actually got married, it didn't last long.

Everyone had his or her own version of the story, but Scott told me that his wife had cheated on him. One day, they had gotten into a fight, and to spite Scott, Elizabeth opened the front door in her bra and panties. Furious at seeing Elizabeth only in her underwear, Scott pulled an old, black cast-iron frying pan from under the kitchen sink and hit her over the head with it, rendering her unconscious.

That should have been my first clue that Scott could possess abusive tendencies. But like any other young, unseasoned girl, I felt that Elizabeth had obviously provoked him and deserved what she got.

4

Witchcraft Comes Alive

The first time I ever went to Scott's house, and he opened the door, there seemed to be at least fifty burning candles, red candles. Although I didn't immediately think about it, the last place I saw a burning red candle was at Werewolf's party. I would also find out the purpose for lighting red candles.

The houses in Scott's neighborhood were constructed tightly together, with beautifully landscaped flowerbeds and vineyards, the sound of constant Portuguese chatter and the smell of Portuguese soup vapors and fried *chourico* (pig intestines) escaping from the kitchen windows.

The house itself seemed pretty ordinary in nature. As you walked in, to the left, was a wood-paneled living room. To the right was a small kitchen and bathroom. Down a small hall, to the left, was the master bedroom, and to the right was a storage room or another small bedroom. Scott's furnishings were basically mix-and-match, comprised of things people had given him after the divorce. However, there was one particular piece that sent chills up my spine when I first encountered it. It was this lamp molded in the shape of an ancient Indian princess. The eyes and mouth appeared as if they were sealed shut. The lamp looked so lifelike. I'm not actually sure why I found this lamp to be so repelling. It was actually a beautiful, elegant lamp. But nonetheless, it gave me the creeps.

This definitely wasn't a room I wanted to be left alone in. Who would have known I'd end up living in the house. Well, after Scott and I went out a little over two years, Scott asked me to marry him after he found out that I was pregnant. However, during the seventies, it wasn't uncommon for girls to marry by eighteen.

Being a modern woman of the seventies, I had to think seriously about whether I wanted to marry Scott or not. I knew that I was more than capable of raising a baby on my own, for I had always been strong-willed and determined. Also, for the past several years, I had aspirations of being an actress. I had taken acting classes all through out high school. I felt that if I married Scott, my dreams of becoming an actress would not come to fruition. However, Scott assured me that I would still be able to follow my dream, and so the story goes.

Since Scott already had a house, we decided to stay there for awhile. It was so reasonably priced. Even though Scott and his ex-wife lived there as husband and wife, for some reason, it didn't really bother me. Maybe it's because I felt that there was no real love lost in that relationship. At that time, I was a senior in high school. I had already acquired a significant number of points to graduate, and as a result, only needed to attend school in the morning. Life was fabulous! I would eat out every day at fast food restaurants, which at that time, were still very new and appealing.

It was a mixed blessing that I had eight months of morning sickness, because Scott ended up doing all the housework. I never had so much attention in my life! But that was all to change. When I was about six months pregnant, unusual incidents started to occur. For instance, as a gift, my mother gave us a beautiful statue of the infant Jesus. Catholics believe this statue can be used to protect your home. So I placed the statue in my living room, facing our front door, as it was custom to do. Several hours later, I was sitting on the other side of the living room watching television, when all of a sudden the statue slid off the end table and fell to the ground. When I got up to retrieve the statue and assess the damage, to my horror, I discovered that the head was completely broken off.

The whole incident was weird because no one had been anywhere near the statue. There were no sudden movements made. The statue was positioned in the middle of the table and just seemed to mysteriously slide and fall. Also, when I gingerly picked up the statue's body and head, I noticed that the break at the neck was clean and even.

When I told my mother what happened, she immediately went out, bought another statue, and had it blessed by the priest. Again, like the first statue, it was only in the house hours before it slid, fell to the ground and sustained a severed head. This time, I didn't tell my mother about the broken statue; I simply put it away in my bureau draw.

By this time, my mother and father had permanently separated. My father moved in with that same young girlfriend from the original affair. My mother ended up moving out of my grandparents' house into a rented house apartment closer to town. Unfortunately, my mother, being the nervous person she was, never learned to drive, so she didn't get out much except when I came over to visit or take her out. So my mother really didn't have an opportunity to come to my house very often. Therefore, I was able to hide the broken statue.

Now I really started to wonder, what caused both of these statues to fall and break? There were no other damages other than the broken heads. What did this mean? I was soon to find out.

The first night it happened, I woke up in the middle of the night feeling like someone was watching me. I looked over at Scott, who was still peacefully sleeping to my left. As I gazed at my bedroom door, I felt every part of my body tense up in horror, for I saw a full outline of a human frame.

As I tried refocusing my eyes in an effort to see this figure more clearly, I noticed it was a man. And it wasn't just any man—it was SCOTT. He was staring at me. It was impossible, for Scott was still sleeping beside me. For a brief moment, I thought about Jack's early childhood incident when he saw himself in the bathroom. I tried to regain composure by covering my head and telling myself it was only my imagination. As I slowly pulled the covers back down over my head, Scott was still there, standing in the doorway.

After several minutes went by, not feeling as frightened, I looked at Scott, who was silently standing at the door. The expression on his face was concerned and somewhat sorrowful. The figure never moved, never blinked. It just stood there silently watching me. I thought for a moment that maybe I was dreaming. So I tried the old "pinch test." It stung, and I realized that I was definitely awake.

Now that I was able to control my horror and fear, I simply went back to sleep. By this time, I was sure that this apparition was not going to move. I think it's because I knew that this figure of Scott was not going to try and hurt me. It was as if he had assumed the role of my guardian.

Throughout this whole ordeal, I never tried waking up Scott. Actually, I never even thought about it. Of course the next day when I told Scott about the incident, he blew it off as a bad dream. Part of me thought it was as well, until several nights later. Once again, I awoke during the night. I looked over at Scott, who was soundly sleeping. I paused for several minutes, fearful of what I might see at the door. Finally, forcing myself to look at the door, I saw another man. This time, it wasn't Scott; it was my brother Ted. At the time, I hadn't seen Ted in awhile. He had been living in North Carolina with our sister Mary. However, to my horror, Ted was at my bedroom door, except he wasn't silent. Ted stood at the door, pulling clumps of hair out of his head. As he continued to intensely rip out his hair, blood was streaming down his fingers. All Ted could silently mouth was "Help me, help me." This time, I did scream for Scott to wake up and as he did, Ted disappeared.

When I told Scott what had happened, his reaction was not one of disbelief. His face displayed a look of concern and now fear. In light of the strange things that were happening, Scott thought he should inform me as to what had transpired in this house before I moved in. As we lay in bed, Scott re-explained that he and his first wife had ultimately split up because she was having an affair. As a result, Scott said that he was consumed with bitterly intense feelings of anger and betrayal. By law, Scott knew he couldn't physically hurt her, although he wanted to, but thought that maybe he could punish her using another method. So Scott purchased several books on witchcraft and spell casting. Scott had decided that he was going to cast a spell on his ex-wife and make her suffer. Scott had no idea why or how he came up with this idea. At the time, he thought it was a great idea, and the best part of all is that his ex-wife would never know that he was the cause of her inflictions.

Needless to say, I was in shock, and for so many reasons. First, based on my past experiences with "the bus witch," this was all too familiar. Second, with Scott doing any type of witchcraft reading, and especially incantations, innocently or otherwise, he had brought evil into this house. Evil that was not going to leave anytime soon. It also made me wonder if Scott himself was actually a witch, or some other evil entity. Maybe he was pretending to be innocent in his knowledge of spells and witchcraft. And lastly, I had to wonder: if Scott was capable of carrying out something of this magnitude, what could he possibly do to me?

I was now able to put two and two together. This was the reason why Scott had so many burning red candles the first time I went into the house. I had read somewhere that red candles are often used when reciting incantations. Scott flipped on the light, got out of bed, went into the closet and pulled out the books. Scott tried handing them to me, but I wouldn't touch them. I insisted that Scott get rid of the books that very night. Unfortunately, I knew throwing those books out was not going to end the evil that possessed that house.

Scott assured me that it was a stupid thing he did in a moment of anger, and that it didn't mean anything. But it did mean something, and it was going to affect all of us. Then, a horrifying thought came to mind. That witch on the bus, on my way to North Carolina, said that she would eventually meet me, even if it were in a different form.

COULD SCOTT BE THAT SAME WITCH? Somehow, I was able to quickly dismiss that thought. Scott seemed more like an unsuspecting victim than an actual witch or devil. The next morning, as I sat in my kitchen having breakfast with Scott, there was a knock on my door. Scott and I usually didn't have a lot of visitors and we certainly had no visitors that early in the morning. Not having a peephole in my door, I was just going to have to open it and see who was on the other side. To my complete surprise, it was my brother Ted. Ted, who I had seen standing in my doorway the night before. Ted, who I hadn't seen in several years.

Ted told me that he needed a place to stay temporarily. Mary couldn't afford the rent for her apartment and had to move in with a friend. Thankfully, Ted certainly didn't resemble his look-alike who was at my bedroom door last night, pulling his hair out of his head. My next thought was: had Ted's spirit detached itself from his body to seek out my assistance? When it was assured of my support, had his spirit encouraged the body to follow? Ted had nowhere else to go. My mother's rented house apartment was just too small. Was this the reason for last night's visit?

Ever since I arrived at this house, I seemed to now be susceptible to all types of unexplained, paranormal activity and with each day, it was only increasing. Ted stayed with me a short while, and when Mary was back in her apartment, he was gone again. It had been at least a month since seeing Ted standing at my bedroom door, so I assumed that was it for the visitations. But all good things come to an end.

That very night, after Ted left for North Carolina, as I opened my eyes, there was Scott standing at the doorway, watching me again. Even though it had happened several times, I was always startled and frightened to see someone standing at my doorway. I wondered what would have happened if I actually stood up and walked over to the figure. Although I contemplated it for a few seconds, needless to say, I was too afraid to attempt walking over to the door.

One night, several weeks after Ted left for North Carolina, as I cautiously pulled my comforter down, I saw another relative standing at my doorway. It was my sister Jane. When Jane appeared to me, like Ted, she was standing at my bedroom door, pulling gobs of hair out of her head. As she did, blood was streaming down her fingers. All Jane could silently mouth was "Help me, Help me."

Unfortunately, with the trauma of my father's departure from our home, Jane had run away, and I also hadn't seen her for several years. The following week, one late afternoon, I heard a knock at the door and when I answered it, there stood Jane. Besides being in trouble with the police in Chicago, Jane had now gotten involved with drugs and alcohol and needed my help. So Jane stayed with me for several weeks. It was good to have her around, especially with me in my eighth month of pregnancy and Scott working all day. But Jane ended up back on the run again and I was alone.

Did the spiritual announcements of Jane and Ted's visits have to do with some type of telepathy? I wondered. For the remainder of my pregnancy, whenever I woke up, I continued to see Scott vigilantly standing at my doorway. It was funny how I never saw more than one apparition at a time standing in the doorway. For the rest of the time that I stayed in that house, only Scott silently stood at the doorway. The expression on his face continued to be that of concern and sorrow.

If that were the only thing that happened to me in that house, I would have been grateful!

5

Confrontation with the Devil

One of my most memorable moments of sheer horror came when I was just entering my ninth month of pregnancy. Even though it was almost twenty-seven years ago, I can clearly recall that it was a Monday night.

As a part-time job, Scott had joined the National Guard. For Scott, who was a Section Chief, National Guard duty was usually a weekend job only. However, Scott was called in for a special meeting, which I thought was strange because he had never been called in previously for a meeting.

When Scott left, I put on the television and sat back on my couch. I couldn't believe that in a few short weeks, I would be having my baby. Scott and I had already decided that if it was a girl, we would name her Cassandra. I just loved that name. Ironically, I would find out later that the Greek goddess of prophecy was named Cassandra. But if it was a boy, Scott wanted to name him after himself. The baby's name would be Scott Andrew Mendes III.

As I continued daydreaming about the baby, out of the corner of my eye, it looked like something was moving. My living room wasn't that big and didn't have a lot of furnishings. Basically, our furniture consisted of a beat up black-and-white sofa bed that was missing half the material, a wooden coffee table and a chair that Scott's mother gave us that needed a cover to hide the holes. To the right of the chair, sitting on the end table, was that Indian princess lamp that I described earlier.

Well, as I quickly scanned the room, my eyes fixed on the object that was moving. It was the lamp. The lamp with the sealed eyes and mouth. To my utter astonishment, the eyes had unsealed themselves and were moving from left to right. The lamp didn't actually move, just the eyes. The eyes were not only moving but the lids were now blinking as well.

Somehow I managed to pry myself from the couch and slowly stand. With my eyes fixed on the lamp, I got up and walked backwards towards the telephone, never allowing myself to move my eyes off the lamp. By the time I reached the telephone, the lamp's originally sealed mouth had now opened. Protruding out of the mouth were large, sharp teeth.

As my trembling fingers dialed my mother's telephone number, I kept feeling like I was going to faint. Although it felt like an eternity, my mother finally picked up the phone. First, my mother tried to assure me that it was only my imagination. She asked me to close my eyes and count to thirty seconds. She assured me that when I opened my eyes again, the lamp would be back to normal. However, I was afraid to close my eyes. What if that thing attacked me? Somehow, my mother managed to convince me that if I closed my eyes, the vision would go away. Well, I did close my eyes for thirty seconds and opened them again. The lamp's eyes were still open and the teeth still ferociously set positioned to attack.

My mother then suggested that I walk over to the lamp and touch the eyes and teeth. Again, she assured me that if I actually went over to the lamp, the eyes and teeth would go back to normal. With my mother hanging on the phone, taking baby steps, I watchfully crept over to the lamp, which was following my every move. Even though the lamp had an opened mouth filled with teeth, it never spoke.

As I slowly lifted my unsteady hand to touch the lamp, in an instant, all the lights went out in my house. As I ran screaming like a mad woman out of the house, leaving my front door wide opened, I realized that the whole town's lights were out. My mother lived only about a mile north of me at the time. Although I was nine months pregnant, I continued running wildly and blindly up the side streets. Unfortunately, I also had night blindness and couldn't see a thing. As I ran, I couldn't help but wonder if someone or something was following me. After what seemed to be an eternity, I approached the apartment house my mother lived in. Wheezing, I could barely climb that narrow, pitch-black hallway that lead to her upstairs apartment. As I entered my mother's candle-lit apartment, I was overcome with joy at seeing the familiar, loving faces of my family. I was safe! I had made it alive!

Before I go on with my story, I'd like to share with you something odd that has just happened.

As noted in the Preface, I've been employed with a large medical insurance company for many years and have been fortunate enough to work remotely from home. Therefore, I have my own office, which includes two desks, a company computer and a personal computer.

Before I begin work each day, while I'm still in an uncluttered state of mind, I continue writing my story on my personal computer. Over the past several days I noticed that my computer seemed to be acting strangely. My mouse was shaking uncontrollably. My computer was also no longer accepting any of my commands. Then, something happened that never happened before, my two-year-old computer suddenly died. I tried every novice troubleshooting technique I could think of to restart the computer, but to no avail; it didn't work. Finally, someone from our IS department diagnosed the problem. He said it was a hardware problem and I would be unable to recover any of my files. That meant every document, including this story, could not be recovered. Unfortunately, I didn't save any documents on diskettes. That meant all my files that contained this story were permanently destroyed. Normally, this would have truly caused me to stroke out if it hadn't been for the fact that I was smart enough to print out a paper copy of this story just several hours before the death of my computer.

Did I say me! Not me! If God didn't put it in my mind to print this document, it would have been lost! I normally never make copies of anything. Like other green computer operators of today, I believed that nothing could ever happen to my documents as long as they were in the computer.

I didn't print any other documents, just this one. But why this one? Why, because I am now convinced that God wants my story told. The devil tried hard to destroy all my work. This is a story that the devil does not want told.

Although I have not yet talked about God's power and influence in my life, it will eventually be revealed.

I've always been a firm believer that one has to open their eyes to see. Even the blind can see what's important. No, I don't mean using your physical eyes to see. I mean using your "spiritual" eyes, which everyone has but which not everyone uses. If you allow yourself to truly see, what you will see might not always be glorious and angelic. Seeing with "spiritual eyes" means seeing evil and good regardless of whether scientists or intellects want to believe these things exist.

It is so easy to dismiss something that you have the inability to physically see or the insight to interpret. So, with God's grace and support, I will continue. However, all of my work will now be pencil-written until I get my new computer. When my new computer arrives, I will have the tedious task of retyping everything I've written.

What makes this so much more real for me is that, just as my computer broke down, I was coming to the most critical part of my life's encounters with evil.

I will continue writing my story using this font to reflect the time that I was required to hand-write my story verses being able to type it directly on the computer.

Now, back to the story. When the lights came on about 10:30 that night, my mother and brother Jack walked me home. Since I refused to go inside, they went in first and assured me it was safe.

Although I didn't want to look, I had to. My eyes immediately fixed upon the lamp. To my surprise, the eyes were closed as tightly as ever, and the mouth was still sealed.

I thought my mother and Jack would look at me as though I were crazy, but they didn't. They knew that for whatever reason, I had truly seen this lamp with eyes and teeth. It wasn't my imagination.

Minutes later, Scott arrived. As I explained my story, Scott tried to quickly attribute it to me being pregnant and overtired. Looking back on the whole situation, I'm sure that Scott felt incredibly guilty for his part in inflicting evil on this house and us. By quickly dismissing the incident, he could relieve himself of the guilt.

Did I mention that I've taken five psychology classes in college? I possess just enough information to make me dangerous! You'll notice throughout my story, I try analyzing out-of-the-ordinary situations. There are no psychological answers to substantiate these bizarre occurrences.

Anyway, my first thought was to immediately get rid of the lamp. But if I did, evil would be victorious over me again. So I decided that the lamp would stay! Fortunately, there were no other "lamp" occurrences, at least none that I was aware or part of.

During July of the bicentennial year, Scott Andrew Mendes III was born. Scotty was a well-proportioned, beautiful nine-pound, nine-ounce baby boy. Scotty had raven black hair, oval sapphire, cat-like eyes (a family trademark except that mine are hazel-green) and the longest, black paintbrush eyelashes I've ever seen. He was just gorgeous! Fortunately for Scotty, he kept his large cat eyes as he became an adult. However, they would change from a sapphire blue to a sapphire blue/green combination.

After my hospital stay was over, Scott, Scotty and I returned home.

Before Scotty was born, Scott and I had turned the spare bedroom into a nursery. Because we didn't have much money, a friend gave me a used crib, which I cleaned up. However, I bought a new mattress. After my own personal experiences with a problem mattress, I thought it would be safer. I also purchased a cheap dressing table as well as other baby necessities.

Unfortunately, back in 1976, they didn't perform routine ultrasounds that determined the sex of the baby. All along, my obstetrician staked his reputation that, based on the speed of the baby's heart, it was a girl. So I foolishly decorated the nursery in a girl's motif. After Scotty was born, I quickly changed the room's appearance.

However, when Scotty first arrived home, he was placed in a cradle that was given to us. The cradle was put in our bedroom. Scotty stayed with us for the first three months.

During those first three months, Scott, Scotty and I had settled into our new family life, and everything was quiet on the home front. Scott had gotten a full-time job at a local shipyard as a ship fitter. He also kept his part-time job with the National Guard. Scotty adjusted like any normal baby, by keeping us awake at night and sleeping during the day.

All of our relatives were just thrilled with him, except my mother-in-law. I couldn't put my finger on it, but she never seemed to be too excited about Scotty. My mother in-law had two granddaughters that she simply doted on.

I was always trying to rationalize why she didn't seem to care for Scotty with such enthusiasm.

Maybe it was because Scott had the same name as the alcoholic husband she detested. Because of this, maybe she was displacing her anger and resentment on Scotty. See, those psychology classes really did pay off.

It was probably because her favorite child and daughter was the mother of the girls. I can recall how she use to tightly lock her arms together while holding Scotty as her piercing blue eyes blankly stared at him.

Later on in the story, my mother in law's "affection for her boys," or lack of it, will be revealed.

But her lack of affection for Scotty didn't matter. Everyone else loved him. When Scotty was a little over three months old, the day finally came. Scotty was moved from our room into his new crib and bedroom. As previously mentioned, this was a small house, so Scotty's room was literally right next door. With the baby monitor on, Scotty spent his first few uneventful weeks in his new surroundings.

However, one late-October morning, as Scott and I sat at the kitchen table having our usual cup of coffee before he left for work, it happened. As Scotty lay soundly asleep in his crib, Scott leaned over, kissed me goodbye and headed toward the front door for work. Almost instantaneously, as the door shut, and Scott's Ford Fairlane backed out of the driveway, my house immediately filled with both male and female people and spirits. Actually, I never really figured out whether they were spirits or people. There were so many of them tightly packed throughout my entire house, I couldn't even move. We were squeezed together like cattle.

These people or spirits were in constant, quick, unrecognizable chatter with each other. It was deafeningly loud. They were all dressed in a one-piece, off-white, basic shroud. No one had yet even observed my presence.

Suddenly, out of the crowd, a short, small-framed man with a burnt-orange complexion and no eyebrows, eyelashes or any body hair, sauntered over to me. The man had an air of confidence and coolness about him. He was not dressed in a shroud. He was wearing some kind of a suit. If it wasn't for the missing body hair, he would have looked like an average, short, and nondescript man. However, I did notice that the crowd parted to let him by. They also reverently bowed their heads. It reminded me how everyone at the party had bowed their heads when Werewolf paraded by.

As he approached, his first words to me were, "Do you know who I am?" And I did! He was the epitome of evil itself! The devil, Lucifer, whatever the name you want to give him! He asked, "You don't recognize any of these people, do you?" I just stood there, terrorized, yet at the same time, feeling defiant. The devil proceeded, "These people are all the devils that will try obtaining your soul for me throughout your life. You will be a great prize indeed!" He went on, "Although you see their faces now, you will not remember a single one of them when you return." Return? Return from where? Where am I!!

Just then, complete panic surged through my body. SCOTTY! He was alone with all of these devils in our house. Although it seemed like an eternity, I was eventually able to push and squeeze my way through the masses into Scotty's room.

There were devils that had joined hands and formed a half circle that surrounded Scotty's crib. They were swaying from left to right and chanting in an unrecognizable language. As they moved back and forth, I saw the farmer musical mobile dancing around and around all by itself. However, for some reason, they couldn't seem to get close enough to the crib. It was almost as if they were forced to stand several feet away from it. I believe that the innocence and holiness of a new baby would not allow them the opportunity to penetrate Scotty's personal space.

As they stood in their perfectly formed circle, they began extending their arms and hands forward. They were trying desperately to reach and touch Scotty. It was as if their very survival was dependent on it. Just as I pushed and shoved these entities, clearing a path to the crib, I suddenly felt a more immediate sense of urgency. I felt compelled to leave Scotty's room and immediately return back to my own bedroom.

As I entered my bedroom, in utter shock, I saw myself laying face down into my bed with my arms and legs spread out by my sides. As I looked at my lifeless body, I had an overwhelming feeling that it was imperative that I immediately return back to my body that instant, before it was too late.

Just as I was going to make my first attempt to re-enter my body, I felt someone grabbed my right ankle, trying to pull me back to the ground. As I turned around, it was the devil, which was in a loud, piercing fit of laughter as he continued to yank my ankle.

Almost automatically, I started screaming over and over for God to help me, and as I did, the devil was forced to let go. As I felt myself slide back into my body, it started to convulse uncontrollably, thrashing back and forth. After the tremors stopped, I was somehow able to force my eyes open. I lay there a few minutes, unable to move. As I slowly regained movement throughout my body, I slid off the bed and onto the floor. After several minutes, I stood up and walked around the house to find that everything was back to normal. Just moments ago, the devil chatter was deafening and now I awoke in complete silence.

The first thing I thought of was: HOW DID I END UP IN THIS BED! Then, I immediately ran into Scotty's room to make sure he was all right. He was still quietly sleeping away, just as I had left him earlier.

As I contemplated the situation over and over in my mind, a thought came to me. The devil that appeared to me was Werewolf, and those people, dressed in shrouds, packed too tight to move, were the nude people at the party. They were back and still pursing me!

After I told a number of people about the incident, the first question I got was, "Are you sure you didn't go back to bed and dream this whole thing?" NO! NO! NO! I didn't go back to bed!!! I was sitting at the kitchen table when Scott got up and left for work!!! Surely, I would have remembered walking over to the other side of the house and going back to bed.

Some people, considered to be clairvoyant, did classify my incident, with the devil, as a very significant out-of-body experience. The environment was sure conducive to an "out-of-body" experience given the fact that Scott had brought evil into the house by practicing witch craft.

It happened almost twenty-seven years ago and I can still remember every specific detail as if it had happened yesterday. But I guess you don't easily forget an experience like that!

Shortly after that incident, my mother, Ted and Jane moved to North Carolina to be closer to my grandmother, aunt and uncle. I was now alone in Rhode Island with no immediate family.

6

Witch Number Two and the Fortuneteller

Shortly after that horrendous experience, I decided to take a trip with Scotty to visit my mother. This was only my second trip on an airplane. Needless to say, I was apprehensive.

Fortunately, it was a cool but bright, autumn-leaf-colored October day. A spectacular array of burnt orange, candy-apple red and lemon yellow colors graced our Rhode Island native trees. It was a breathtaking ride to the airport.

As I said my goodbyes to Scott in the airport, I bravely walked into the plane with Scotty. Scotty looked so cute dressed in his faded blue-jean overalls, red plaid shirt and little work boots. I must say, he was simply adorable.

I overcame the first hurdle by walking on the plane. I found my row and window seat. To my surprise, the plane was virtually empty. It was wonderful. As I was settling myself into the seat and new surroundings, I became aware that a man had quickly sat beside me. Since the plane was empty, I wondered why this man had decided to sit beside me. I then remembered that passengers were not allowed to change their seats until after the plane's door was closed and it was preparing to depart, so I appeased myself with that explanation.

However, even after the door had closed and several people started changing their seats, the man beside me did not move; he didn't even budge. He just sat there staring straight ahead. As the plane started ascending and eventually leveling off, people once again began walking about the cabin or moving into empty seats. But again, this was not the case with the man who sat silently beside me. After awhile, I stopped thinking about it.

When the stewardess (they hadn't been renamed "flight attendants" yet) had just finished passing out drinks and snacks (otherwise known as peanuts), the man beside me began to speak.

With a too-pleasant smile and a melodic, almost entrancing voice, he started making small talk. He asked me questions like, "Have you ever been on a plane before?" "Where are you going?" "Do you work?" etc. So, being my polite self, I replied to his questions with short, to-the-point statements.

However, it wasn't until he asked me how old Scotty was, BY NAME, that I realized something was wrong. I never told this man that my son's name was Scotty. I knew that the "slip up" was intentional, because the man's eyes had maneuvered themselves onto mine. That now apparently fake smile had also returned to his face.

Before I could respond, although only a fraction of a minute passed by, I quickly studied the man's make-up. He had to be somewhere in his late forties or early fifties. He was at least six feet tall, with an unexercised body frame. The remaining hair that encircled his head was grayish-black. Lines had already deeply consumed his face. His blue, marble eyes were set back abnormally deep into his face. However, his smile was perfect. Those teeth were as even and bleached white as possible. Actually, they didn't match the rest of his worn face at all.

After my brief assessment was complete, I sharply asked him how he knew that my baby's name was Scotty. The man reply, "I know everything about you and your family, Mosqeet." Where had I heard this before! A dreadful, familiar feeling came over me.

The man proceeded to provide me with my husband's name, where we lived etc. But what really astounded me is when he talked about my "bus encounter" from number of years earlier. He confidently said to me, "Consider this visit our second attempt to persuade you to change your mind about joining our cult.

"I, like that woman on the bus, am a witch. We both belong to the most powerful cult in the world, which is located in New York. And I, like the other witch before me, have been sent to persuade you into joining us."

It's amazing that even under extremely stressful situations; your mind can be think of other things. For instance, he mentioned that this was a "second attempt." What about the Werewolf and devil visits? Shouldn't this be the fourth encounter? He only referred to the "witch on the bus" visit and this one. Why didn't the "bus witch" or this "plane witch" connect themselves to the devil? Unfortunately, that question would never be answered.

He went on to say, "Your potential power and ability surpasses that of the average witch. If you would agree to allow us help develop and refine your power, greatness and much authority will be yours throughout eternity. Actually, we would help to develop you powers—and Scotty's, for he has also inherited the necessary abilities. Scotty will also have the full ability to transfer and receive."

Although completely caught by surprise, I was able to respond quickly. Maybe it was because I had already been exposed to a number of supernatural incidents. Therefore, in a confidant, strong voice, I told him that, as with the witch before him, I was not interested in his proposition. I adamantly stated that I was a strong Catholic who believed in my religious convictions. God was the master I chose to follow and to his commands alone would I respond.

He tried to convince me that my church was disloyal and didn't want me because I had been married to Scott by a Justice of the Peace. Scott was married the first time in the Catholic Church and until his marriage was annulled, we couldn't be married there. Therefore, the Catholic Church did not recognize our marriage.

However, I shouted, "That was a lie! It was actually I who was disloyal to the church. And even so, my church did not abandon me, nor did I abandon it. Although it's true that the Catholic Church didn't recognize my marriage, they still loved me, and so does God. Just because a child does something wrong, a parent doesn't stop loving them."

As my voice became even louder, as loud as possible in an airplane without drawing attention, I replied, "I denounce the devil. I want nothing to do with him or you—ever!"

The man's smiling face had now turned dark and stern. As his abnormal eyes grew wider and the vein on the right side of his neck pulsated, in a low, almost non-audible voice he replied, "Hold fast to your convictions, Mosqeet, for when an opportunity presents itself, we will be watching and waiting for you and Scotty."

As I started to recite "The Lord's Prayer," the man quickly moved to a seat far from mine. I didn't stop praying until I arrived in North Carolina. Unlike the "bus witch," he didn't disappear from the plane. Actually, he just got up and walked off normally, never looking back.

As I gently picked Scotty up from his seat, I could still feel my entire body shaking. As I stepped off the plane, I was so happy to see my mother. However, my mother had enough of her own troubles, so I didn't want to burden her with yet another extraordinary occurrence.

So, as I had with every other incident, I tried to quickly dismiss this one. This ended up being easier than I thought. I didn't have another incident until Scotty was about two. And actually, it wasn't a real incident; it was more like a "proclamation."

My husband's sister, Jacqueline, was having one of those "parties" that you were guilted into attending and where you were forced to buy overpriced items you knew you could get for the half the cost in a regular store. Jacqueline had the party at my mother-in-law's house. Actually, it was a gigantic apartment.

My mother- and father-in-law had rented the second floor of an original New England colonial home built around 1700. It had been successfully converted into two enormous apartments.

Unlike today, back in the 1970s, this was not considered chic or indicative of great wealth. Quite the contrary, it signified people who couldn't afford anything else. My father-in-law's drinking left them in financial ruin, and they lost the new house that they'd purchased several years earlier.

When they first moved into the apartment, the attic had to be cleaned. While Scott and I were cleaning the central section of the attic, we came across several paperback books on the topic of witchcraft. We both stared at each other and placed the books in a garbage bag. As we worked in silence, it was obvious that we both knew that this was no coincidence. However, neither one of us verbalized our thoughts. In the future, my mother-in-law would move into two other houses that also had witchcraft books in the attic. Were they left by previous tenants, or were they actually her books? I was sure Scott knew the truth. It also made me wonder if my mother-in-law was the one to put Scott up to "casting spells" on his ex-wife. Scott never did confirm that to be true.

Anyway, the apartment was beautiful. It had grand roman columns with high cathedral ceilings in every room. Each room was double the size of what would be considered a normal-sized room today. The only small room in the apartment was the very narrow kitchen.

Jacqueline's party was being held in the living room. To make the party more interesting, and I'm sure with the motive of increasing attendance and potential sales, my sister-in-law hired a fortuneteller.

As fortunetellers go, this one put on the usual show by providing each girl with tidbits regarding their past and present happenings. Fortunetellers never seem to be able to tell you about the future, or at least I thought.

The fortuneteller eventually went through all the girls but me. That was fine with me, however, since I had no desire to have my palm read or anything else. My mother had drilled it into my head that having your fortune read was inviting evil in. It was also against my religion. But the girls insisted it was only for fun and no harm could come of it, so reluctantly, I agreed.

As I sat down near the fortuneteller, she studied me for a few moments and appeared to be uneasy about reading my palm. However, it wasn't until she actually touched the palm of my hand that an alarming look appeared on her face.

The fortuneteller immediately dropped my hand as if she had received an electric shock from it, got out of her chair and swiftly moved away from me. I was left sitting alone, perplexed.

The girls were just as surprised as I was. Frightened, I asked the fortuneteller what was wrong. Continuing to move away from me, in a low, silent voice, the fortuneteller said, "Intense evil surrounds your aura. You will experience much misfortune, heartache and unhappiness throughout your life. It is actually too terrible to reveal. It will be very difficult for you to overcome. I'm not sure you'll have the strength to endure or survive."

With that, the fortuneteller said she had another appointment and had to leave immediately. The fortuneteller was in such a tizzy that she left without being paid. It was apparent that she didn't want to remain around me.

Strangely, the fortuneteller did not make this kind of prediction to the other girls. Why me! I suddenly felt like an outcast. All the girls were staring at me in bewilderment, except my mother-in-law. She actually looked quite pleased and not surprised at all by what the fortuneteller had revealed. It was almost as if she subconsciously planted the suggestion in the mind of this woman.

7

Not Even Death Stops Mrs. Mendes

As stated earlier, there was something about Scotty and I that my mother-in-law didn't like. Her dislike was very obvious whenever she was around Scotty. I always had this feeling that she was jealous of Scotty for some reason. At first, I thought she was jealous of his beautiful facial features, which were unlike those of her other grandchildren. However, it always seemed like something else was making her jealous, but I couldn't put my finger on it.

When Scotty was born, she never came to the hospital or my house to see him. As a little boy, she would buy him the lesser gifts of all the grandchildren. After the movie *Damien* came out, Damien became her favorite new name for Scotty. I couldn't understand it. It wasn't as if he were a mischievous or evil child. But nevertheless, she was relentless in her persistent ridicule of Scotty. I would later suspect that she might have been jealous over Scotty's "potential abilities," which would far surpass her own. So it was no surprise to me when she sided with her daughter Jacqueline when the babysitting incident occurred.

My mother moved back to Rhode Island, from North Carolina, when Scotty was about two. After finishing two years of technical college, I was now working in a doctor's office as a medical assistant. While I worked, my mother agreed to baby-sit Scotty.

It so happened that in the summer of Scotty's fourth year, my mother decided that she wanted to take a week's vacation to visit my grandmother in North Carolina. Therefore, I needed to find another babysitter. Jacqueline was already home with her two daughters, so she agreed to watch Scotty, naturally, for a price. Because Jacqueline lived rather far from us, Scotty was sent to spend the entire week, including the nights.

When Scott and I went to pick up Scotty at the end of the week, not only did he look like he hadn't taken a bath in a week, but only one outfit was sent home to be cleaned. I wanted to give Jacqueline the benefit of the doubt, but Scotty himself innocently told me that he hadn't changed his clothes or taken a bath even once.

Needless to say, I was furious and argued with Jacqueline over the incident. Of course she adamantly denied it and called Scotty a liar. Somehow, that fight resulted in us not speaking to each other for almost three years!

However, because Jacqueline was my mother-in-law's favorite daughter, she sided with her, and I ended up not speaking to her for almost three years as well. Although, my husband still went down once a week to see his mother, and rightfully so. However, Scotty and I did not accompany him.

Unfortunately, my mother-in-law got sick during that time. I believe it all started just before Scotty was born. My father-in-law ended up having seven small heart attacks, at the time, one after the other. Miraculously, this prompted him to end a lifelong drinking. Overnight, he transformed into a completely different man, a model citizen. He became a recruiter in the Air Force and joined a number of charitable organizations as a volunteer.

As a result of my father-in-law's miraculous transformation, my mother in-law, who had endured a lifetime of anguish because of his drinking, could not stand the thought of everyone now thinking he was so wonderful. So she ended up taking on his persona and inadvertently became an alcoholic. However, she was able to cleverly disguise her drinking problem. Every afternoon, she would go into her bedroom, pretending to watch soap operas. However, she would always take a quart of vodka with her.

Sadly, she ended up with severe cirrhosis of the liver and was told that, even if she stopped drinking, she would have at best only five more years to live. However, I believe she had a kind of death wish, for her only sister had recently died, as well as her mother. She had no remaining relatives from her "first family." She was obviously depressed and didn't care about living. Although my father-in-law tried helping her, she managed to find a way to obtain liquor and continued drinking.

It was only months later, two days before Mother's Day to be exact, that my husband received a call from his father informing him that his mother had been rushed to the hospital, and that it didn't look good.

Although I was now feeling extremely guilty and remorseful for not speaking to her for almost three years, I decided not to go with him to the hospital. When my husband returned home that afternoon, he told me that my mother in-law pleaded over and over for me to come and see her.

ME! Why me? Even when we did speak, we really didn't get along. My husband and his family were surprised too. Maybe she did have hidden feelings for me after all. My husband also told me that the doctor said she was dying. Needless to say, if someone's dying wish was to see me, I would certainly be willing to put all grudges aside and make amends.

Unfortunately, by the time I arrived at the hospital, it was too late. My mother-in-law had lapsed into a coma. As I watched her jaundiced, bloated body being kept alive on a respirator, I couldn't help but wonder why she wanted to see me. What would she have talked about? Would she have apologized? Would the message have been entirely different altogether? Maybe, she would have revealed the truth about herself.

In any case, that night, I had what I'll refer to as a prophesizing dream. A prophesizing dream is a dream that either comes true or has a purpose or meaning related to an event that will occur in "real life," one that will eventually reveal itself through the course of time. It was like the black cloud mist dream I had as a child.

Anyway, I dreamt that my two sisters-in-law (who were married to my husband's brothers) and I were sitting on the left-hand side of my mother-in-law's dining room table. My other three sisters-in-law (my husband's sisters) were sitting on the right hand side of the table. My father-in-law was sitting at the head of the table. My mother in-law's seat had been intentionally left empty.

My father-in-law pulled out a crumbled, piece of torn notebook paper and started to read. It was my mother-in-law's will. As far as I knew, nothing like that really existed. As he read her will, I wondered why her sons weren't at the table.

As my father-in-law continued reading, I looked to my left to see my mother-in-law standing near her favorite daughter, Jacqueline. Although I saw her, I knew she was dead. But no one else acknowledged her presence. But as my mother-in-law stood near my sister-in-law, all she could do was shake her head in silence. As she shook her head, filled with sorrow, she began to cry. Why was she crying? And why was I part of this will reading anyway? I awoke out of the dream to the sound of the phone. It was my father-in-law calling to inform us that my mother-in-law had just died. I felt bad that I had not had the opportunity to speak with her again.

By now, I had attended a number of funerals and viewed a number of bodies. For the most part, people have a look of peace and contentment on their faces. However, as I gazed at upon my mother-in-law's stone-cold body at funeral parlor, I could never recall anyone looking so angry. Her eyes were almost frowning and her lips were tightly molded to her face. I swear she looked as if she were gritting her teeth as well.

Anyway, after the wake and funeral were concluded, we went back to my father-in-law's house. My father-in-law had asked that my sister-in-laws and I be seated at the dining room table. His hand was pointing to the left side of the table. Then, he asked his daughters to sit on the right-hand side.

This set-up was looking all too familiar. My father-in-law then pulled out a sealed piece of paper from a plain white envelope. He stated that my mother-in-law had written her will just days before she died. The will contained a list of her personal belongings, which were to be immediately distributed to her daughters and daughters-in-law. My father-in-law said that even he didn't know the contents of the will. He was told not to open it until my mother-in-law was cremated and buried. He had explicitly followed her last wishes. Oh my God, my dream was coming true!

My father-in-law first addressed my oldest sister-in-law, Tory. My mother-in-law was never close to Tory, and it was reflected in her inheritance. Tory was left some old jewelry that was worth nothing, not even sentimentally. The youngest daughter, Kami was then addressed. She was left my mother-in-law's car and washing machine. How odd, I thought. But then I realized that this was an ironic slap in the face. You see, Kami abused everything my mother-in-law owned. Kami lived upstairs in an apartment my in-laws created for her and her son. Kami use to take my mother-in-law's car out on the weekend to the clubs. That car had been in more accidents and left abandoned more times than I can count. It ended up turning into a piece of junk. Supposedly, the washing machine was the same. Anyway, the day my mother-in-law died, both the car and the washing machine also mysteriously died. Therefore, Kami was only left with my mother-in-law's items that she herself had turned into junk.

Her favorite daughter, Jacqueline, was saved for last. Therefore, my youngest sister-in-law, Tammy, who was married to my husband's youngest brother, was next. Tammy, another non-favorite of my mother-in-law's, was left her very expensive pearl and diamond earrings. I noticed that my father-in-law hesitated when reading the item. The expression on his face was that of shock and disbelief. Because he wasn't allowed to look at the will until after the funeral, he had inadvertently put those earrings on my mother-in-law as part of her burial outfit.

Unfortunately, my mother-in-law had requested to be cremated. There went Tammy's inheritance, if you'll excuse the tasteless reference, "up in smoke!"

My other sister-in-law, Ronnie, who was married to my husband's middle brother, Wayne, was next. Ronnie got all the things she had given my mother-in-law back, which also amounted to insignificant trash.

I was next! What torturous thing did she have in store for me? I was her least favorite daughter-in-law, who hadn't talk to her in three years. As my father-in-law proceeded to read that I was to receive her entire doll collection, everyone in the room, including myself, was stunned. My mother-in-law's doll collection was worth thousands. If she had just written her will days before she died, why would she leave such a valuable collection to me?

My father-in-law hesitated only for a moment and went on to read what was left for my mother-in-law's favorite daughter, Jacqueline. Jacqueline was left all kinds of wonderful things: an exquisite grandfathers clock, antique furniture, expensive jewelry—everything that truly had worldly value—except the dolls.

Then it occurred to me why my mother-in-law was crying and shaking her head in the dream. I believe she realized that this daughter had only sucked up to her, during life, in an effort to obtain all of her earthly treasures after death. My mother-in-law provided Jacqueline with the most affection of all her children. She wouldn't even give any of her other children a chance to demonstrate their love. Her only interest was Jacqueline's happiness and well-being. I believe the dream signified her realization of the horrendous error made at her children's expense. I suspect that she felt somewhat sad, and perhaps foolish.

However, the question still remained, why did she leave me her dolls? My first thought was that this might have been a grand gesture to make amends. Why would she want to do that? She never, ever liked me. And then it hit me! Of course!! The Portuguese believed that evil entities had the ability to put their spirit or other spirits into the bodies of dolls. If my mother-in-law was actually involved in any evil activities, as I believed she was, perhaps her gift was intended to provide me with a lifetime of torment. I know it sounds ridiculous, but there was no other logical explanation.

I wasn't about to keep those dolls. I was overwhelmed with the desire to get rid of them before they had a chance to enter my house. I told my husband that I wanted to give them to her granddaughters. That is where they rightfully belonged. My husband was dumbfounded. He knew how expensive those dolls were and felt that I should keep them. But I refused. They were mine to do as I pleased, and I decided to give them away.

Even though Jacqueline had gotten practically everything worth any real value, she was still more than willing to accept the dolls on behalf of her daughters. After giving those dolls away to Jacqueline's daughters, I thought that would be the end of my doll dilemma, but it was only the beginning.

After my mother-in-law's death, the days and months seemed to move at a normal pace. However, by August, it was evident that my father-in-law had a girlfriend. She unexpectedly appeared at his 60th birthday party. It was strange—I could have sworn I also saw this woman at my mother-in-law's funeral. There had been a lot of speculation that he had been seeing this woman before my mother-in-law's death. Then I thought, maybe my mother-in-law wasn't crying because of Jacqueline, but actually over my father-in-law's indiscretion.

Anyway, before I knew it, the holidays were flying by. It was obvious that my mother-in-law was no longer around, especially at Christmas. There was no longer someone spending an exorbitant amount of money on her grandchildren—with the exception of my son of course, not that I'm bitter or anything. All of the children and grandchildren got equal amounts of everything, which wasn't much. My father-in-law was having too much fun spending my mother-in-law's life insurance.

Well, winter left and spring arrived right on time. One spring evening, I had another one of those "prophesizing" dreams. It wasn't merely a dream containing a special meaning or an insight into a future event; I felt as if the conversation were actually taking place at that very moment. It was similar to an out-body-experience.

My mother-in-law and I were facing each other surrounded by nothing but darkness. My mother-in-law was dressed in one of the shrouds she used to wear years before, when Scotty was a baby. She spoke angrily at me.

"Where is my doll?" she shouted.

I confidently replied, "What doll? I gave all your dolls to your granddaughters."

She grew increasingly aggravated. "You have my dolls, and I want them back!"

Again, I strongly replied, "I have none of your dolls."

Now shouting, she replied, "The English Mother. I want the English Mother doll."

Horrified, I realized that she was referring to the doll my father-in-law had given me for Christmas. With conviction, I said to her, "Dad gave that doll to me for Christmas—it didn't belong to you, and it was a brand new doll."

Now, in a strangely sarcastic, low voice she replied, "Just look at the tag, look at the tag." With that, the alarm was ringing and I woke up.

With my heart still beating fast but aware of my surroundings, I quickly glanced directly across the room at the hope chest my husband had made for me years ago. There, sitting all alone on the top of the hope chest was the English Mother doll. She was a porcelain doll dressed in nightclothes representing the mid-1800s period. She had a nightcap that was tied around her head. She sat there holding a tiny baby that was also dressed in clothes from the mid-1800s. The doll had an unusual mouth, neither smiling nor frowning, kind of like a *Mona Lisa* smile. Although sitting, the doll was being held up by a stand. Nothing about her had changed since the dream. However, I was now afraid to touch her, fearing that my hands would catch fire or explode. Anyway, I eventually mustered up the courage and picked her up.

My mother-in-law had instructed me to "look at the tag." There were no visible tags, for surely I would have noticed them when I had gotten the doll for Christmas.

After examining the doll's external garments, I started to search through the layers of petticoat. Still, there was no sign of a tag. However, I would not feel comfortable until I was absolutely sure that doll did not belong to my dead mother-in-law. So I decided to undress the doll completely. The petticoats were first. Again, no tag was found. The nightgown was next. Just as I started to lift the nightgown over the doll's head, it got caught. As I started to probe around, I felt a piece of cardboard. Instead of lifting the dress over the doll's head, I went in from behind. As my hands held on to the doll's torso, I could feel the piece of cardboard, so I quickly retrieved it and pulled it out. The tag said, "Happy Mother's Day." Happy Mother's Day—what did this mean? I had received this as a Christmas gift.

While sitting a few minutes with the card in my hand, a strange thought came over me. I ran to the phone and called my father-in-law. I asked him if the doll he had given me for Christmas once belonged to my mother-in-law.

My father-in-law seemed startled, but he replied, "It didn't actually belong to your mother-in-law. I was supposed to give it to her for Mother's Day, but with her sudden death just two days before the holiday, I never had the chance. I knew you liked dolls, so I decided to save it and give it to you for Christmas." He explained further, "It wasn't a used doll or anything. Your mother-in-law didn't even know I had it." Naturally, he wanted to know why I had asked such a question. I told him that I just noticed the Mother's Day card inside the doll's nightgown and was curious.

As I hung up the phone, my mind was racing. One thing I knew for sure was that that doll was history. Once again, I gave the doll to Jacqueline for her daughters. I knew that if the doll was in her granddaughters' possession, she would inflict no harm on the girls.

I've never had another dream about my mother-in-law since that one. Although I wonder all the time, what happened to her? Where did her spirit really end up going? Sometimes, the people you think are "devils" really aren't.

Was she one of those devils that were gathered in my house the morning of my first out-of-body experience, or was she just an unfortunate woman who couldn't handle some of the extreme challenges of life? I guess I'll find out someday. But for now, I can only ponder over the experiences I had with Mrs. Mendes.

Other than Mrs. Mendes, I did have other significant dreams in that house. For instance, I had a dream that there were three small children in a tiny, run-down apartment. The children were screaming in agony, as their bodies seemed to be burning from the inside out. The next day, there was a story on the news that three kids, who had been left alone, in an effort to keep themselves warm, turned the blower of a gas stove on without the pilot being lit. They died of asphyxiation. I also had a dream that I was walking in New York City with my young niece. I noticed a big crowd in a frenzy of excitement. As I got closer, I saw that everyone was looking up to the sky at a tall building. At the top, I could see a man holding a gun to an elderly woman's head. Fearful that my niece would see this tragic event, I grabbed her by the hand and started running the other way. However, when I stopped running, I found my niece and myself at the top of the same building where the incident was unfolding. Actually, we were standing directly behind the gunman and the elderly woman.

All of a sudden, the man shot the elderly woman point blank in the right side of her head, at the temple. Suddenly, everything was in slow motion; the elderly woman's head detached itself from her body. As it did, I could literally see her brains and blood exploding out of her head.

With one hand on the elderly woman's shoulder, the man took the gun, put it in his mouth, and pulled the trigger. As with the elderly woman, I also saw his head detach and separate from his body as they both slowly and silently drifted toward the floor.

Once again, the very next day, there was a story about a political figure that, while on stage to address his audience, opened his brief case, pulled out a gun, put it in his mouth and pulled the trigger.

Although these types of dreams didn't come true exactly as I'd had them, the underlying motifs did.

I did have other dreams that came true, but which were not as significant. For example, the doctors I worked for once asked, at the last minute, if I would be able to register some doctors they had invited as they arrived for a reception the following evening. So, during the day, I tried to get an emergency hair appointment for the next day over the lunch hour.

I knew this would be virtually impossible because of the popularity of this hairdresser. In fact, there were no appointments. However, she did put me on a waiting list. That night, I had a dream that my hairdresser called me to tell me that she had a cancellation and could see me after all. The next day, that is exactly what happened. The strange thing about the situation was that this hairdresser had never had cancellations. She had found it odd that someone cancelled an appointment over the lunch hour, which was an extremely difficult appointment to obtain. I did wonder whether the cancellation had to do with someone simply canceling, or if there was more behind it. Was it possible that I could make my desire for wanting that person to cancel an actual reality? Was this an example of the power those witches spoke of?

Of all the dreams I had in my life, besides the one about Mrs. Mendes, the most significant was a dream I had about Scott. I had a dream that Scott and I were standing on top of a steep mountain cliff. In between us stood the devil. Ironically, it was the same man that I encountered during my out-of-body experience. All of the evil spirits/people that had crowded in my house that day also stood on this mountain top.

The devil spoke to me and said, "If you promise yourself to me, I will allow Scott to live."

Although I feared for Scott, I said, "No, I will never give my soul to you for anyone." The devil then gave a quick glance at Scott and, seemingly in severe pain Scott immediately started to fall to the ground.

Now infuriated, the devil said, "Don't you realize I have the power to kill him?"

I wondered why he didn't threaten to kill me. I replied, "God is more powerful than you."

Again, the devil gave a quick, fixed glance to Scott. This time, Scott gave a gut-wrenching cry and fell to the ground. As the crowd stood in constant chatter, the devil said, "I am done requesting your soul. I now demand it! If you don't give your soul to me now, Scott will die."

All of a sudden, a euphoric, whirlwind feeling consumed my body. With every fiber of my being, I loudly and boldly screamed out, "God help me, God help me!" The more I screamed, the stronger I felt. And as I proclaimed God's name, the devil and his cohorts disappeared over the mountainside. Scott slowly stood up now freed from the devil's torments.

This dream was so real it actually prompted me to go and speak to a priest friend of mine. The priest told me that the dream had a definite significance. The priest's interpretation of the dream was that Scott was being manipulated by the devil, directly or indirectly, and couldn't free himself without assistance.

The priest felt that, although I was trying to be helpful to Scott, only he could release himself from the devil's manipulation. Because of Scott's weaken state, and his predisposition to evil, the priest also felt that the devil was using him in an effort to get to me.

As I sat back and reflected, I could see the pattern of manipulation unfold throughout our married lives.

8

Angel of God, My Guardian Dear

Although so much darkness had consumed our lives, especially when we lived in that house, there were rays of hope that reminded me that God loved me and was protecting me. When Scotty was about six, in an effort to save money to purchase our own house, I got a part-time job at a local department store, in the shoe department. I was already working a full-time job at the time. In order to get to the shoe stock, I had to climb twenty-nine small, steep stairs to the storage room.

On one evening, with five pairs of shoe boxes toppled high within my hands, I started to descend the stairs. As I did, I could feel that my right foot had completely missed one of the stairs. To my utter dread, simultaneously, my left foot also slipped off the stairs. In a fraction of a second, both my feet were airborne. As I watched the shoes fly out of the boxes and fall to the ground, I knew that once I finished falling down those steeply-spaced twenty-nine steps, I was going to be seriously injured or dead.

All of a sudden, I felt a soft burst of air gently lift my body and place my feet back on the stairs. Both my feet had been replanted firmly on the steps. Even the shoes that had fallen were back in their boxes, sitting in their original positions in my hands.

As I swiftly looked from side to side and front to back, I couldn't find my rescuer. However, I didn't really have to look. I knew who had come to my aid. I believe that we have guardian angels that watch and protect us. Although this was the first time I had ever witnessed such blatant evidence of my guardian angel's existence. I silently prayed a prayer of thanks. For without my guardian's angel's assistance that day, I truly believe I would have died.

For the rest of the evening, a euphoric feeling consumed me. What a special gift I had been given that evening. Once again, I was able to witness God's works by allowing myself to see with my soul instead of my eyes. I decided that I would not try to create an unlikely logical explanation, and would simply accept the truth.

This incident would be one of many I would witness and acknowledge with my "inner eyes."

9

The Italian Stranger

Well as you can see, I just got my computer back! No more manual writing for me. That's why I'm now typing with my regular font and size. Hooray!!! Let's see how long it lasts.

Unfortunately, my marriage to Scott was doomed from the start. Our breakup had nothing to do with the spiritual evil and misfortune he had indirectly bestowed on our family. It was physical, tangible evil that destroyed our marriage: alcohol and physical abuse.

Almost from beginning, Scott abnormally resented Scotty. I'm not sure what the reason was, other than the fact that Scotty initially took a lot of my time. This resentment seemed to intensify along with his alcohol consumption. Basically, to make a long story short, Scott physically abused me whenever he drank. Any little comment would set him off. It was during this time that I realized Elizabeth probably had valid reasons for leaving Scott.

Scott tried hard to intimidate me, because I was so young and impressionable. He would threaten me with comments such as, "If you ever try leaving me, I'll kill you." Scott, being a Vietnam veteran, once stated that he found it easier to kill people than to hurt animals. Therefore, I really believed that he was capable of killing me.

Fortunately, a lot of my "battle scars" were hidden and no one ever knew the violence that was occurring behind closed doors. However, I would have never allowed Scott to lay a hand on Scotty. That's where I would have drawn the line.

Unfortunately, although Scott did not abuse Scotty physically, he did very much so emotionally. In every picture ever taken of Scotty and Scott together, they're standing a foot away from each other, with Scott either expressionless or frowning. Scott's lack of attention to Scotty also significantly contributed to his behavioral problems in school and at home. Although Scotty was extremely popular with the kids, and eventually the ladies, he still exhibited symptoms of low self-esteem. Even though I tried to make up for the loss of his father's attention by being both father and mother, it didn't work. Scotty's behavioral problems seemed to be escalating, so by the time he was ten, I started taking him to see a psychologist. Of course, Scott was not interested in attending the sessions or in what the psychologist had to say.

As my overall unhappiness grew, I felt that I needed and deserved the comfort of a man that would really love Scotty and me. Still fearing that Scott would kill me, I was able to convince myself that becoming a "cheater" was acceptable in light of my unhappy circumstances. It was easy to justify my behavior with this kind of rationalization. However, after several affairs, I found that this was not the answer either. It was when I intentionally stopped looking that it happened.

Up to now, although I had lived my entire life in Rhode Island, I had never gone ten miles outside of my hometown into other parts of the state. Most other people who lived in Bristol never traveled that far as well. However, on the night of June 17, 1988, my whole world was about to change forever. Some friends of mine invited me to a nightclub in the town of North Providence. I was definitely leery.

The ethnic culture of North Providence was predominantly Italian. Growing up in a predominately Portuguese part of the state, we were warned about Italians. Portuguese thought of them as a backstabbing people that couldn't be trusted. The Italians felt the same way about the Portuguese. Later, I would find out that the two cultures probably resented each other because they had so much in common.

Not too far from North Providence, Italian Mafia occupied a section called "Federal Hill." If people tell you that the Mafia doesn't exist, don't believe them. I would later discover that the Mafia does in fact have an extremely strong presence in Providence.

The surroundings of North Providence resembled that of a small hillside village in Italy. There were shops that sold nothing but Italian pastries, meats and cheeses. Neighborhood houses were adorned with colorful flowerbeds, grape vineyards (used for homemade wine) and well-endowed Italian women garden statues. It was a page right of out an Italian vacation guide.

The nightclub we were going to wasn't that far from Federal Hill. It was located to the north of a congested Italian populated neighborhood. I would later learn that my future prospective in-laws lived to the north of this night club, about a block away. My friends had chosen this club because their favorite disco/pop-rock band was performing. When we arrived, the club's seedy, weather-beaten look on the outside remarkably resembled that of the inside.

It was a miracle, but we managed to find a table and chairs. What surprised me even more was that we could find a table and chairs at all. It was so dark in there I couldn't see anything. After arriving at my table, I finally acclimated myself to the surroundings. It was nothing special: your local drunks, middle-aged women with over-processed hair trying to pick up young guys, old men trying to pick up young girls, and last but not least, big-haired glamour girls waiting to be fawned over but planning on going home with no one. Just when I determined that this club was occupied by the usual bar crowd, I turned to the back of the club and headed towards the bar, which was about twenty feet away.

For several moments, I found that I had forgotten how to blink. My eyes were fixed on a man who was at least six feet tall (I would later discover he was 6'2"), with chestnut, golden-layered shoulder-length hair and small, cowboy-eyes including long eyelashes and a long, classical-Greek-structured face. Although he had a pronounced nose, it seemed to fit perfectly with his neatly-trimmed mustache and bearded face. His body was large and solid. I also noticed a tattoo on the lower, outside part of each arm. What did these tattoos signify? Strength? A "bad-boy" persona? A motorcycle gang? What? This intrigued me.

To me, he was utterly breathtaking. Until now, having been exposed to only your basic Portuguese man, he definitely had a very different look about him, one you would not forget, or want to forget. If I were to guess, he definitely looked Italian. He sat at the bar talking with both his mouth and hands to someone who appeared to be his friend, and his friend's big-haired girlfriend. After several minutes of observing the conversation, the girlfriend slapped her boyfriend in the face and stormed out the door. The Italian Stranger thought it was funny and started laughing at his friend, who immediately pursued his girlfriend out the door. After they were gone, he turned to another guy on the other side of him and started to talk. I don't know why I was so fascinated with this man, but he certainly caught my attention, although he never noticed me.

I eventually refocused my attentions on my friends, and our night commenced. I had such a good time. The band was really good. I had a blast dancing and socializing. During the mid to late eighties, it was still all right for girls to dance fast together without anyone thinking anything of it. Today, people think girls are lesbian if they dance together.

During that time, I had hoped that the Italian Stranger might ask me to dance, but he didn't. I spend a good part of the night turning down men who asked me to slow dance. I was always appalled when a man I didn't know asked me to slow dance. I always felt they had an ulterior motive. I'm not saying I was special, either—they were asking every girl in sight to dance.

It was an hour before closing and the Italian Stranger was still at the bar. This time, I noticed one of those late middle-aged, over-processed blondes trying to pick him up. I watched her buy him a drink. For some strange reason, I felt betrayed. As I continued to stare, his friend spotted me, shoved the Italian Stranger and pointed my way. Before I could successfully retreat, his eyes caught mine. He didn't exactly smile, but an intrigued look came over his face. I quickly turned around. He hadn't danced with anyone all night, and now the second-to-last song was playing. I decided to turn around for one more look. As I turned around, he was now staring at me.

If I were to select the most memorable moment in my life, this was it. He looked at me, cocked his head down to his left shoulder, and with his left thumb, flipped it toward the dance floor. Could it be he was asking me to dance without ever leaving his seat? It certainly would save someone the humiliation of being turned down.

To my delight, it was a fast dance! I was absolutely fascinated. Although my friends were mortified that I would even entertain the idea of dancing with him, I nodded my head "yes" in reply. He was now walking toward me. My heart was beating abnormally fast. As he moved his hand along my body, guiding me to the dance floor, I was amazed I remembered how to walk.

When the Italian Stranger and I started to "dance," I realized he must have really wanted to meet me, because he couldn't dance to save his soul! When the dance was over, he came over to our table started speaking with me.

My ears recognized the sound as speech, but what kind of speech, I had no idea. After he said a few more words, I analyzed the accent. It was a cross between heavy East-Coast and twenties Mafia gangster. Oh no, I thought! How could that voice be coming from his mouth?

He introduced himself as Wayne DePasquale. Wayne asked me if I wanted to go to the packed, greasy diner across the street for breakfast. It was already 2:00 a.m. and I feared that he wanted to do more than eat, so, as intrigued as I was, I declined! I was married and was tired of being a cheater, so I politely said "No." I would later learn that he really just wanted to get something to eat.

Wayne then asked my name and impulsively, I said Robin. Robin was the name I used when I didn't want to give out my real name. Although I was interested, I was also afraid. But not too afraid to give him my business phone number. I figured if he was really interested, he'd find me. Actually, the emotional part of me wished he would call, while the common sense part of me wished he wouldn't. Therefore, I left it up to fate.

After he left, my friends fervently begged me not to have anything to do with him. Because of his appearance, I think they feared he might be abusive. However, if you saw both Scott and Wayne together, you would have never guessed that clean-cut Scott was the abusive one. I also suspect that subconsciously I thought, because of Wayne's physical appearance, he would be able to protect me from Scott. Could it be possible that Wayne was strategically placed in my life to help me escape from Scott? In any case, I felt extremely connected to him!

Well as Mondays do, it arrived, and I was back at work. During the day, while talking with one of my staff at her desk, my administrative assistant informed me that there was someone on my phone looking for a "Robin." She proceeded, "When I told him there wasn't a Robin at this extension, only a Mosqeet, he started to describe this Robin, and you seemed to fit the description."

Although my initial reaction was excitement, it was coupled with fear. I really didn't know this guy. What was he really all about? Was there a reason he was crossing my path now? Was this another trick of the devil? I knew I had to be cautious. Maybe the average person wouldn't have entertained the idea that Wayne might also be a servant of the devil, but my life had been far from average, therefore, the thought did cross my mind!

I nonchalantly said I would take the call. Trying not to appear as if I was running, I quickly went into my office and shut the door. When I said hello, the voice was unmistakable. Wayne's first question was, "Why did you tell me your name was

Robin if it was really Mosqeet?" Calmly, I told him that he must have misunderstood me, even though Mosqeet definitely doesn't sound like Robin.

Wayne seemed to accept the explanation. He then asked me if I wanted to go on an air balloon ride with him. I was stunned by the offer. No one had ever asked me that question before. Without going into detail, Wayne could tell I had reservations, so he counter-offered by asking me if I would join him for a drink in a very public restaurant or pub. I agreed! The restaurant we chose was located far from where I lived.

The next night, we met at the restaurant. It was only a matter of time after Wayne began conversing that his deplorable accent seemed to diminish. I found out that he was currently working as a roofer. Unfortunately, it would be only one month later that Wayne would sustain a severe, debilitating spinal cord injury. Although the injury didn't leave him paralyzed, it left him in a lot of pain. I also discovered that he was divorced (from a cheating wife and lousy mother—I could only imagine what he would think of me) and had sole custody of his son, also named Wayne (who was seven at the time).

Wayne made suggestions that he had minor connections with the Mafia. Apparently, when he was younger, he was "driver" for some local Mafia members. However, it sounded more like a bodyguard job to me. Apparently, after Wayne was born, he got out of that line of work.

His love for his son impressed me. Here was this massive man, with long hair; tattoos and an earring, yet so devoted to his son. So unlike Scott, Mr. American Vietnam Vet! This was obviously a gentle and sensitive yet strong and very masculine man, possibly the perfect package. It was now my turn to tell my story. Wayne was amazingly empathetic. By the end of the night, we had agreed to continue meeting, just as friends.

I think we were at a local amusement park when I actually fell in love with Wayne. Wayne was so full of life, so adventurous—everything Scott was not! Wayne was someone who had no problem showing affection, not so much verbally, but physically. Wayne opened up a part of me that had been dormant for many years. Unlike Scott, Wayne was only one year older than me. At this time, I was three months away from my thirtieth birthday. I found that I had so much more in common with him.

I also discovered that Wayne owned a new Harley Davidson motorcycle, but had actually been riding since he was sixteen years old. He was definitely exciting. I was discovering that we complemented each other's personalities very well.

Unfortunately, the situation with Scott and Scotty had gotten worse. During our last session with the psychologist, he had informed me if I didn't leave Scott he was going to call Social Services and have Scotty permanently removed. Scotty had become extremely rebellious and resentful.

Since the day he was born, my son had been my life. Therefore, without hesitation, I made plans to leave the house. On the psychologist's suggestion, I secretly found an apartment, hired movers and left one afternoon, never to return. I did leave Scott a detailed note that included my reasons for leaving and a list of every terrible thing he had done to me—to us—from day one.

Unfortunately, it wasn't until the shock of me leaving after almost fourteen years of marriage that Scott turned his life around. Even though I begged him for years to go to counseling, it wasn't until after we left that he actually started to see a psychologist. However, he was too late where I was concerned. I was already falling in love with Wayne. I do give Scott a lot of credit. He was able to eventually resume, or I should say begin, a normal, healthy relationship with Scotty.

After I moved into the apartment and divorced Scott, Wayne and I got very close, actually inseparable. We took all kinds of spur-of-the-moment trips and motorcycle rides, and attended all kinds of festivals, shopping malls, casinos and of course, amusement parks. When our children were finally introduced, they got along incredibly well. Wayne was so good with Scotty. He was genuinely interested in him and what he had to say. It's sad, but this was the first time that Scotty actually conversed in a positive manner with a "father figure."

Meeting Wayne's parents was interesting, but a pleasure. I was invited to their home one Sunday afternoon for dinner. When I walked into their two-tenement house, it was exactly how I had envisioned it. They occupied the first floor. The family room and living room were tastefully decorated in an early-Victorian motif, but it still had an Italian look. Maybe it was the laced kitchen tablecloth or the smell of sautéed garlic coming from the kitchen.

There was a bowl on the table overfilled with ravioli and gravy (spaghetti sauce to us non-Italians). There was also a salad seasoned with vinegar and oil and of course, Italian bread. Wayne's father even brought out the special-occasion wineglasses.

Although Wayne's mother was tall, this wasn't the first thing I noticed about her. She had the clearest, olive, porcelain-textured skin and beautiful thick hair. Wayne definitely got his height from his mother's side of the family. However, Wayne had the exact same face of his father with the exception of his father's sparkling blue eyes. Wayne also had his father's dry sense of humor. They were both refreshingly delightful. Although they were Italian, they did not match my mother's stereotyped description. It was unfortunate that my mother and her parents had probably encountered a number of "cruel" Italians that left a bad taste in their mouths.

Wayne also had three brothers. However, the oldest one lived in Arizona. The other two lived in New England. Those two also joined us for dinner. They also somewhat resembled Wayne.

I can vividly recall Wayne, his two brothers, his father and myself sitting at the dinner table. It wasn't until Wayne's mother sat down and finished preparing her plate that the rest of them started to clean out the remaining ravioli, salad, and bread. It was amazing! The pace was fast and furious. It was so startling that I couldn't move. However, Wayne made sure to put in a few raviolis and a piece of bread on my plate. The meal was fabulous, and Wayne's parents were very nice. They were completely different than my ex-in-laws.

After meeting Wayne and his family, I felt even more connected. In all aspects, I felt that I had truly found my soul mate! The soul mate I had searched for all my life! I felt that God had truly smiled upon me. Maybe with all the bad things that happened, my ray of sunshine would be here to stay.

It wasn't long before Wayne and his son moved in with Scotty, my mother, our dog, Ritchie, and me. Of course, because we weren't married yet and being brought up very Catholic, Wayne slept on the couch. The only reason my mother didn't have a fit that Wayne moved in period was because he had proposed to me and we were to be married. Everyone made sure to give me their opinions as to why I shouldn't get married just after divorcing, but I was always someone who did exactly what I wanted, which wasn't always necessarily a good thing.

It was Christmas Eve morning when Wayne came running into the apartment announcing that he had found a house for us to buy. Wayne had made an appointment for us to meet the construction owner and look at the inside of the house.

The house was located in North Providence, Wayne's hometown. However, Wayne told me this was coincidental. When I walked into the house, I couldn't believe my eyes! It was gorgeous! It had a half-moon window at the top of the front door and a big bay front window in the formal living room. The carpets in the family and living rooms were mauve. It also had a spacious kitchen and two bedrooms and bathrooms on the second level. There was also an enormous master bedroom. As I entered this room, I felt air rushing in and out of the unoccupied space that surrounded my body. It was such a peaceful feeling.

Although the basement was unfinished, we looked at it anyway. Wayne had proclaimed himself quite the handyman and assured me that it could be easily refinished. As I entered the basement, I assumed that my feelings of being surrounded by hidden evil were back only because it was dark. I would find out later that my feelings were founded.

Outside the house, there was also a large porch with a long staircase that went down to the ground. It was a house that I knew we couldn't afford. But Wayne, being a shrewd bargainer, talked the owner into substantially reducing the price. Apparently, Wayne acquired information regarding some financial trouble the owner was in. He found out that the contractor needed the money to pay off the loan. Reluctantly, the contractor accepted the offer. Of course, we still had to get the mortgage, but it actually looked like it could almost be possible. This was another example of Wayne's "can do" attitude, making the impossible possible. We closed on the house a day before we got married.

The wedding was certainly memorable. Both of our sons looked sharp in their tuxedos, and they were happy they were going to be real brothers. Both of them had expressed their displeasure at being only children. My sister Jane came up with her infant son, Joseph. Joseph was actually named by me after St. Joseph. St. Joseph was and still is my patron saint and guide. When the baby was born, Jane told me I could name him—so what better name than Joseph.

Joseph wasn't expected to live. Luckily, Jane's baby did not contract her HIV illness. Under St. Joseph's guidance, he was one of the fortunate babies who were able to shed their mothers' HIV antibodies and develop their own HIV-free antibodies. His brother, Michael, who was born a year earlier, was not as fortunate. Joseph was truly a gift from God, with a meaningful purpose in life.

What fitting tribute to St. Joseph to have Joseph baptized at the wedding. My mother, being one of the very few people in my life who always demonstrated genuine love for me, was my maid of honor. It was just as thrilling to have my younger brother, Ted, give me away. Ted had always been there for me during the worst and best times of my life. He was always someone I could count on. Wayne demonstrated his deeply-hidden feelings for me when he cried at our wedding during the exchanging of vows.

Our reception was just as much fun as the wedding itself. We had approximately 100 guests. I wore a satin, creamed-colored gown with a matching Bolero jacket and an elegant hat with a veil. Wayne's black tuxedo and freshly-starched white shirt looked tremendous. After our first encounter with Wayne's "dancing abilities," we stuck to slow dancing the night away, which was much more romantic.

After the reception, we went back to our rented hotel room. We had no money left for a honeymoon. Everything we had was put as a down payment on the house. The next day, we started moving into the house. As I unpacked, there were unavoidable reminders of Scott. I couldn't help but wonder what our lives would have been like if we'd stayed together. I never thought we would ever have divorced. But at least no abnormal occurrences had transpired over the past several years. Maybe the evil reign was finally broken.

10

Jane Meets the "Black Cloud Mist Man."

It's strange that I began writing the "Jane" chapter during the month of August. It could have been any other month, so why this one? As you know, Jane and her infant son, Joseph, had come up for the wedding. However, after the wedding they returned back home to North Carolina. Jane and Joseph were living with Joseph's father, Brian.

However, just about the time Joseph turned ten months old, Jane came back for good to stay with Wayne and me. Jane had realized that Brian wasn't good for her or Joseph. Throughout Jane's life, I found that if her "current" boyfriend really cared about her, she got bored with him. The more a boyfriend didn't want her, the more she wanted him—often to the point of obsession.

As mentioned earlier in the story, Jane became a runaway early in life. Whenever she was caught or found, Jane was confined to a number of behavioral and alcohol rehab facilities. Unfortunately, Jane got involved with heroin and other debilitating drugs. In order to afford these drugs, Jane got involved in prostitution and other illegal activities.

As mentioned earlier, somewhere along the way, Jane was told she was HIV-positive, which would ultimately lead to AIDS. It could have been contacted from Jane's IV drug use or prostitution activities. No one knows for sure, no one ever will.

But no matter how "street-wise" Jane appeared to be, inside, she was secretly scared of not being accepted, an insecure girl who desperately just wanted to be loved. Jane was extremely likable and very charming. But more importantly, Jane was a tenderhearted, compassionate person who would have done anything to help anyone. Jane's feelings ran deep and were genuine.

Once Jane arrived back in Rhode Island, Jane lived with us (in between boyfriends). After a period of time, Wayne ended up renovating the downstairs of our raised ranch into two bedrooms, a living room and bathroom for Jane and Joseph. After living with us for about a year, although she still went out on the weekends and didn't always come home, for the most part, Jane seemed to be doing better.

Jane joined the church choir. She had a lovely singing voice. She was an alto, like me. Jane had even gotten involved with my charity work, visiting the elderly once a week.

Unfortunately, within a two-year period of time, Jane's drinking increased once more and she started getting involved with drugs, like Cocaine, instead of Heroine. As a result, it was in that renovated, downstairs apartment that the "Black Cloud Mist Man" resurfaced.

During this time, it was brought to my attention that Jane was bringing all kinds of men into our house. Drugs and alcohol and God knows what else accompanied these men. Because she had her own entrance, I wasn't aware of what was actually going on downstairs. It wasn't until years later that we discovered everything.

Unfortunately, Wayne II, now in his early teens, and Scotty, in his middle teens, were game for any kind of action Jane was willing to throw their way. Thank God they never got involved with drugs. But they did get involved with alcohol. It was a real party downstairs. Wayne and I didn't realize how much action was going on in that downstairs apartment. Like most people, we had to work during the day and went to bed early at night. Unfortunately, the kids got out of school before we got home, and with Jane on permanent disability, it was a free-for-all every afternoon.

The reason Wayne and I even allowed Jane to move downstairs was because she had supposedly given up drugs and only drank occasionally. We thought it would be a nice opportunity for Jane to get her life in order. Also, it would provide a safe haven and stability for Joseph. In the case that anything happened to Jane, Wayne and I, Joseph's godparents, had agreed to raise him. His father, Brian, had now long been out of the picture. He was also having trouble with excessive drug and alcohol abuse. For all we knew, he could have also contracted AIDS from Jane or someone else.

At times, I just couldn't cope with the thought! I just couldn't believe it! My baby sister, Jane, had a disease that was going to kill her, and there was nothing I could do! But the doctors assured us that Jane was doing remarkably well under the circumstances. In a way, I guess it was good that Joseph spent so much time with Wayne and me when Jane went out.

As the activity downstairs started to heat up, strange happenings began to occur. Although Joseph was only about three years old, he came running upstairs one day, horrified one night that he had seen a "tall black man that looked like clouds." However, his description of the man fit the word "mist" more so than "clouds." He said the apparition had stopped at his bedroom door, looked in, and started floating up the stairs. Even though it was made of "clouds," he could still feel the vibration of the mist moving up the stairs.

Jane didn't tell me about Joseph's encounter with the Black Cloud Mist Man until she had an experience of her own. However, her recollection was much more vivid. The Black Cloud Mist Man fiercely entered her room, and while she was sitting in front of her shiny, black lacquer vanity, the entity enclosed itself around her. The more she tried fighting him off, the stronger he became.

Somehow, Jane managed to get off the vanity bench and reached for the telephone. Supposedly, the Black Cloud Mist Man sent the phone off the flying wall and across the room in a fraction of a second. Jane then tried running out of the room, but when she did, the Black Cloud Mist Man lifted her up in the air and threw her around the room like a rag doll. Interestingly, as Jane was flung around the room, her body never touched the ground. The only item to break in her room was the mirror to her vanity. It was only when she pleaded to Our Blessed Lady and Jesus to come to her aid that the torment stopped.

I know what you're thinking: a child and someone who was probably high or drunk saw this Black Cloud Mist Man. A child's imagination dreamed it up and it was the mother's drunken/drug-induced illusion. I would have thought the same, until sometime later, when my brother Jack also encountered the Black Cloud Mist Man.

Keep in mind that Jack was never told about the Black Cloud Mist Man. We decided to keep it amongst ourselves. However, one day, when my brother Jack, now stationed at a naval base in Newport, Rhode Island, drove up to see us and spend the night, an unexpected incident occurred. Jack was sleeping on a couch in our formal living room, which was located on the second level of the house. Jack awoke to the sound of someone shuffling up the steps that led from the downstairs apartment to the top floor. Although Jack never heard the door open that connected the downstairs to the top floor, he knew that someone or something had materialized in the upper level of the house. As Jack tilted his head slightly to the left, he saw a black mist, with sporadic holes of air, coming toward him. The black mist was approximately six feet tall and had the shape of a disfigured man. Jack, who always carried holy water with him, wet the tips of his fingers and flicked the excess at the black mist. This seemed to slow the Black Cloud Mist Man down, but it didn't stop him. So Jack took off the cap of the holy water bottle and threw it, ensuring that the water would cover a good portion of the Black Cloud Mist Man. This caused the Black Cloud Mist Man to dissipate.

Although Jack told my mother what had happened, I again was not told out of fear that I would be horrified. My family tried to shelter me from incidents such as these because of everything that had happened in the past. Unfortunately, although my family tried to keep me from learning of the Black Cloud Mist Man, I would encounter him again in the not-too-distant future.

11

Signs of Trouble

Wayne and I had completed almost three years of marriage when the first signs of trouble appeared. During those first three years, for the most part, Wayne and I were your typical newlyweds. Well, except for the fact that we already had two teenage sons, my sister, her son and my mother all living with us. Needless to say, it was the perfect recipe for disaster.

Although I had received a medical/secretarial certificate from a technical school, I never had the opportunity to start college after getting married so young the first time, so I decided to go back to school. This is when I took all my physiology classes and is one of the reasons I'm writing this book. I had two English professors that encouraged me to try writing a book after reading my materials.

During this time, Wayne had gotten abnormally involved in his motorcycle and motorcycle friends. Unfortunately, Wayne's back problems were also getting worse. With the numerous prescriptions for addictive pain medication that he was taking, Wayne became someone I no longer recognized.

However, it wasn't until Wayne came back from a motorcycle rally in Florida that it was obvious things had changed. Wayne had just up and quit his job without having another one to go to. Supposedly, it was due to his back problems. However, his doctors did not consider him disabled.

Each day when I returned from work, Wayne would not be at home. I would also discover he had been gone for most of the day. Wayne also seemed much more distant. Our relationship was rapidly spiraling downward at the same rate that it had accelerated, and I had no idea why.

Wayne started going out on Friday and Saturday nights with his newly found motorcycle friends. Every Sunday, Wayne would go out for a motorcycle ride with his friends. I was no longer invited to go. During this time, Wayne and I verbally fought almost daily. One particular night, being a modern woman of today, after one of our fights, I decided that I was going to sleep on the couch. So I took my pillow snatched a blanket from the bed and stormed off to the living room. Of course, Wayne didn't budge. He could care less. It only meant that there was more room in the bed for him!

After I comfortably positioned myself on the couch, I tried to go to sleep, but I couldn't. It was unimaginable that I could have been so happy just a short time ago. My life had become disastrous!

As I lay on my back dwelling on my life, out of the corner of my eye I caught a glimpse of what appeared to be someone walking up from the basement stairs. I couldn't tell who it was. Was it Jane or Joe?

Just as it came around the corner of the stairs that connected to the upper level of the house, I was stricken with terror! I couldn't move, scream or do anything. I thought I was going to die. It was a black cloud mist with gapping holes throughout its body. As it came around the corner, it came after me with full force. It was the Black Cloud Mist Man! Hysterical, I tried desperately to maneuver myself off the couch onto the floor. But black cloud mist had a tight grip that seemed to surround my body. After what seemed to be an eternity, I somehow managed to fall to the floor. I struggled to stand, but the black mist cloud was too strong. The more it hung on to me, the more powerful it seemed to become. I tried pulling, pushing and punching, but to no avail. I couldn't shake this thing.

As hard as I tried, I also discovered that I couldn't scream. No voice would come out of my mouth. Then, I did the last thing I could think of, and that was begging God to help me! I remembered reading a prayer that said, "Ask anything of the Father in my name and he will give it to you." So I pleaded with Jesus, God, Our Blessed Lady, St. Joseph and anyone and everyone to help me.

The Black Cloud Mist Man lessened its grip and eventually let go. It was just enough that I was able to half-run, half-crawl up the hall toward my bedroom door. When I was about halfway up the hall, I could feel both my legs being firmly pulled. As I turned around, it was the Black Cloud Mist Man again; it was relentless. This time, I continued struggling to get to my bedroom door. As it pulled, I pushed forward. When I grabbed the knob of my closed bedroom door, I suddenly felt my legs completely lifted off the floor. I was now levitating in mid-air. I held on to that handle for dear life! The more horrified I became, the more the Black Cloud Mist Man was surrounding and wrapping itself around my body.

Once again, I screamed out for God's help, and once again, the Black Cloud Mist Man somewhat retreated. However, it still had a hold of my feet. Somehow, I managed to turn the door knob and stick my hand inside. Miraculously, as soon as I stuck my hand inside my bedroom, the Black Cloud Mist Man immediately let go. As I fell to the ground, I subsequently dragged the rest of my body inside the room. As I turned to shut my bedroom door, I watched the Black Cloud Mist Man, in what appeared to be a weakened state, shuffling down the hall and back down the stairs.

Now, safely inside my bedroom, my knees buckled and I fell to the ground. I realized that this demonic Black Cloud Mist Man was forced to let go of me once a part of my body had entered my bedroom, a bedroom that was blessed with holy water each night, a bedroom that contained numerous religious statues on my bureau top. There was too much "holiness" for this dark, evil creature to endure. For if this Black Cloud Mist Man had somehow attached itself into me, it would have been able to immediately feel the holy aura and religious presence that surrounded this room.

Even though I knew this Black Cloud Mist Man had headed for the downstairs, I wasn't about to go warn anyone. However, it didn't matter, for I had a feeling that it was living and thriving downstairs. Unfortunately, I'm sure that there were enough evil acts going on downstairs to keep it alive.

Being the reflector that I am, I thought back on the other time that I had seen this Black Cloud Mist Man. As you may recall, it was when I was a small child, in the hospital, when I had that dream about floating in boat down the dark river and watching the Black Cloud Mist Man running along the sides. Although I'm sure that most people can feel evil in one form or another, i.e., anger, hatred etc., not many actually get to confront it in its physical form.

To my amazement, Wayne never woke up. The whole experience terrified me so much that once I regained control of my legs, I quickly jumped into bed, pulled the covers over my head and held on to Wayne tightly. Even if he didn't seem to care, it made me feel safe.

Unfortunately, Wayne continued to spend enormous amounts of time away from the house. After about a month of this activity, I came home one evening from school to find that Wayne had just come in. Now Wayne's time away from home was spilling over into weekdays and weekends; this had to stop! I was now the only one working, and was unable to keep up with the growing number of bills. That was the last straw! Angrily, I said to Wayne he had no business coming in this late, and I wasn't going to stand for it.

I will never forget his reply. He said, "Actually, I'm glad you brought that up, because I'm not sure that I love you anymore or even want to be with you."

Still being somewhat naïve, having been married all those years to Scott and only having had one other boyfriend, Zach, figure wasn't able to figure out that it had nothing to do with "loving me." Wayne had a girlfriend on the side. But I wouldn't find out about his girlfriend until two months later. When Wayne announced that he didn't think he loved me any more, I never felt such utter devastation in my life. I had loved Wayne so much. Even though Wayne's activities over the past several months would have been obvious to the average person, I just didn't see it coming.

Wayne attributed his loss of feelings for me to our family issues. The fact that my mother lived with us, that Jane and Joseph had moved in, and that our kids were somewhat out of control made him angry. He blamed me for letting it all happen. Of course, until that moment, I had no idea these issues had bothered him so much. However, unbeknown to me, these issues weren't the real reasons for Wayne's betrayal.

After the announcement, I became depressed and distraught. I had lost so much weight that I became dangerously close to anorexic. I didn't want to get out of bed and would sometimes stay there for days at a time. My work was now suffering tremendously. I was fortunate to have such a good staff; they picked up the slack until I got on my feet again. Wayne was still living at the house, but was never home. I literally allowed him to come and go as he pleased. I didn't care, as long as he didn't leave. I didn't want to lose him. What I didn't realize is that I had already lost him.

I tried everything to correct the problems Wayne had brought to my attention, including telling my mother, who had lived with me for the past fourteen years that she had to move. I stopped going to school. I tried setting up romantic dates and exciting activities. I allowed myself to get further into debt by charging anything that Wayne wanted. Unfortunately, nothing seemed to draw us closer. Wayne eventually told me it was too late.

Finally, one day, one of my co-workers called me at work and told me that he had seen Wayne at a fall festival hanging all over some girl with long blond hair and a bandana tied around the top of her head. I was completely crushed! That was the first time I was forced to entertain the idea that Wayne actually had a girlfriend. After finding the love of my life, he seemed so lost to me. So when Wayne returned home, I confronted him with the story, and he adamantly denied it. This "girl" was supposedly the wife of one of his friends, and he denied hanging all over her.

I wanted desperately to believe him, so I did. However, the very next week, after going out on a Friday night, Wayne did not come home at all. He finally came home the next day with a story about falling asleep at his friend's house. Again, I wanted to believe him, so I did. I was grasping at straws. Wayne had also gotten heavily into drinking and multiple narcotic prescription ingestion.

This girlfriend was pure evil herself. I do not say this merely because she was cheating with my husband, or fueling his addiction to alcohol and drugs. No, it was something else. I would find out that even though she had a six-year-old daughter, she got drunk with Wayne every day. She was your perfect party girl. She was everything I wasn't. She had no sense of family, responsibility or religion. She was absolutely horrid.

Wayne's supposed best friend from next door (who was also cheating on his wife) had told me that Wayne was seeing a girl he had met on the motorcycle rally, and that he was making a fool of me. Once again, Wayne denied the story, and tried convincing me that his friend was just trying to get in my good graces, hoping to one day go out with me. Even though my emotional side allowed me to believe Wayne's lies, my brain told me otherwise.

It wasn't until Wayne actually moved out of the house and went to live with his girlfriend that both my mind and heart were forced to come together. Wayne was gone! He had left not only me, but his own son, Wayne II, a child he had raised from a baby all by himself, to move in with someone who was completely wrong for him, someone who was helping him destroy himself.

That's when the real torment began. There was something I hadn't realized before, that devils don't necessarily only come in the form of a "spirit;" they can come in human form. There is much more of an opportunity to succumb to the charms of the devil if a person thinks they're just communicating with another person—a female, in this case. This was the situation with Wayne and this devil.

Whenever Wayne would call the house to check on Wayne II, he was always drunk or high, and she would be swearing and shrieking in the background until he was forced to hang up on me. Then, she would call me when Wayne wasn't around to tell me how much Wayne hated me and my family, using explicit details as her ammunition. She would also tell me what a great lover my husband was, and how much she was enjoying him.

And I let myself play into the trap! The more she told me about Wayne, the more depressed I became thinking that not only did he not love me anymore, but that he despised me. I had become so depressed that I could barely sleep at all. I couldn't stand being in that bed, our bed, alone.

Surprisingly, although remarried, Scott came over to the house several times in an effort to console me. I asked Scotty if he had called his father about Wayne and me breaking up. He adamantly said no. During one of his now weekly visits, I asked Scott how he knew that Wayne and I had split up, especially considering that he, his family and friends lived on the other side of the state. He said he heard it from somewhere. Not really being interested, I simply accepted that explanation.

Scott wasn't my only support. Every night, like clockwork, a three-year-old Joe would climb into my bed and snuggle close to me. He would creep up to my face; gently place a kiss on cheek and say, "He'll be back."

I use to think, how bizarre! How would a three-year-old even have a clue as to what was going on? What made him think that Wayne would be back? As I lay there dwelling on Joe's comment, I remembered something. During this awful time in my life, I pleaded—literally fell down on my knees begging God, Jesus, Our Blessed Mother, and St. Joseph, everyone I could think of to help me. Help me survive this ordeal; help me keep my job, pay my bills, keep my sanity, and most importantly, I begged to have Wayne return to me. I attributed Joe's confidence that Wayne would return to a message from God.

Unfortunately, as the situation seemed to deteriorate, like most untrusting humans, I lost faith. The calls from that witch were daily now! For some reason, I just had to pick up the phone and listen to her very graphic conversations. During this period of time, I tried to resume my life. I dated a very successful electrician who had his own company. He was a handsome, divorced man who was a lot of fun and romantic all at the same time. He had two children whom he adored and demonstrated his love and commitment at every opportunity.

In order to relieve tension, he suggested that I join a gym. It was a great suggestion. It helped to make me feel calmer and tone my body. I had always been on the thin side. However, after all the weight I lost, it was the perfect time to tone up. Unfortunately, we ultimately split up because he knew that my heart was still with Wayne. That I could turn down the opportunity to permanently be with someone so perfect tells me that I must have really loved Wayne. To my surprise, my dating really bothered Wayne. That was confusing. I was getting mixed messages.

It so happened that one day, as I was driving down the highway, I saw Wayne's truck a few cars ahead of me. I decided to follow it in the hopes that it would lead me to the house where he was now living. As he exited the highway, I was closely behind. As he pulled in to a paint-peeled, broken-down apartment building, I just couldn't believe it! He left everything behind for this?

As he got out of the truck, she came down the stairs. It was the first time I had ever seen her. She was almost as tall as Wayne, with a medium to large frame. She did have long blonde hair and wore gobs of make-up. Again, she was everything I wasn't. As she grabbed his arm and started walking toward the house, I couldn't help myself, I pulled my car into the drive way and ran out. When she saw me, she ran up the stairs. However, Wayne remained behind. He was so drunk. Slurring his words, he tried telling me that she was what he wanted. He still loved me but needed her. That was an interesting word, "needed."

As he turned and walked up the steps into the house, I started heading for my car when I hear footsteps racing down the stairs. As I turned around in hopes that it was Wayne, I saw her. As we confronted each other, I could feel the negative energy pushing against my body. I said to her, "Your boyfriend went back upstairs."

She replied, "It's not him I want, it's you. It was never him that I wanted. He was my only connection to you!"

My brilliant comeback was, "What do you want with me?"

She said, "What we've wanted all along, for you to join us. But then again, we're not the only ones that want you." Now I was totally confused.

Suddenly, as I looked into her face, it looked almost as if it had temporarily transfigured into the witch's face on the bus. However, for a few seconds, she also took on the appearance of the man on the plane, the devil that appeared to me long ago, and then finally Scott. She momentarily took on the appearance of all the demons that had so far, taunted me throughout my life.

I became aware of what I was experiencing when her face returned to its original appearance. She was simply smiling. "Yes," she said. "Besides our continual pursuit of you over these years, a curse was recently placed on you. Not actually on you, but on your husband, Wayne. I believe you know who it's from." It only took a moment of thought to realize who had put the curse on Wayne. There was only one person I knew who could "cast spells." It was the person who once practiced witchcraft on his ex-wife, a person who I'm sure wanted to either punish me, hurt Wayne, or both. It was Scott!

She proceeded, "I have the power to end this torment, break that spell, and return your husband back to you right now. Fulfill your destiny, join us! We need you and you need us!"

A rush of emotions consumed me. First of all, I realized that Scott was part of every bad thing that had happened in that house while we were married. However, I still wasn't convinced that he was just allowing himself to be manipulated by the devil. Second, I couldn't believe that I was still being pursued after all these years. I assumed she was referring to the same witch's cult I had been hearing about since I was thirteen. And lastly, I feared for Wayne. He had no idea what he was getting into! Before Wayne met me, although brought up as a Catholic, he hadn't routinely practiced his faith. However, after Wayne met me, he got much more involved in religion. Wayne was interested in what the priest had to say, went to church every Sunday and on holy days and, most importantly, practiced his faith's beliefs, especially kindness and compassion to his fellow human beings. Apparently, he was still vulnerable, allowing himself to be so easily manipulated. It also didn't help that he had a spell cast upon him.

Although I should have felt some type of relief that this woman was some form of evil and not really interested in Wayne, I didn't, because the bottom line was that he chose to be with her and not me. I felt that our love could not have been as strong as I once believed. However, once I got over my emotions, I realized that Wayne was already at a low point in his life. His problems with prescription narcotics and drinking started long before he met her. Besides the constant pain in his back that plagued him day and night, Wayne needed to resolve other issues regarding our family unit and personal life before real healing could begin.

I wasn't even sure that our relationship was something he was interested in anymore. Frankly, I didn't know if I was still interested. But now that I knew that demonic forces were at work, I would now have to fight to help Wayne save himself at the least, even if our relationship was finished. Even if we didn't end up back together, I couldn't let Wayne be taken over by this demon from hell!

It was around Thanksgiving time when Wayne called me at work. I happened to be alone, in my office, when the call came in. "Mosqeet, it's me!" Although it took seconds to say, it seemed like an eternity. I was completely surprised! It was almost like the first time I had heard his voice. But this time I wasn't filled with excitement over the possibilities. I was surprised, because Wayne hadn't called me at work since we broke up.

My first thought was something was wrong. But instead of asking if that was the case, I just asked how he was doing. Wayne said he wanted to tell me a story. He told me that when he woke up yesterday, he had a revelation. He didn't say "revelation," but I knew what he was implying. Wayne stated that for the first time in a long time he felt that what he was doing was wrong. He had deserted his family, his life and, most importantly, a wife that he adored. Wayne said all he could think of doing was going to church to seek God's counsel and support. But he felt that his family, including me, would never forgive him, nor would they want to take him back.

His timing was perfect, for at that very moment, there was a special Thanksgiving mass going on. Wayne said as soon as he entered the church, a wave of complete and utter remorse come over him. As he fell to his knees on the church bench, he began crying hysterically! He told God he just wanted to go home. What I had longed for was finally coming to fruition. Wayne was begging me to come home! However, being only human (I think), I wondered if the only reason he wanted to be with me was because something had happened between him and his girlfriend. Maybe she had broken up with him, or perhaps he had actually managed to break free.

Wayne assured me that she still very much wanted him; he just didn't want her. I would later discover that this was true. I asked Wayne if he wanted to come over later that night to talk over the situation. Wayne quickly agreed.

I guess I thought the first physical contact after our breakup would have been somewhat casual, with generic conversation and neither of us making eye contact. Instead, almost simultaneously, we held onto each other tightly, as if reaffirming that we'd never lose each other again! Following the tight embrace was the most passionate kiss we had ever shared.

We talked a lot that night about what had happened—the problems corrected and those still requiring correction. There was no doubt in my mind that Wayne and I wanted be together, to try once more.

The next day was Thanksgiving, and in my usual fashion, I was feverishly preparing all of the family's usual holiday favorites. Although the kids made sure to stuff their faces to the maximum with food, the holiday was awkward. The kids were so uncomfortable around Wayne. They acted as if he wasn't even at the dinner table. They were also very angry with me for taking Wayne back. I guess I might understand why Scotty would be mad, but not Wayne II. After all, this was his father, who raised him since he was a little boy, alone, long before I came into the picture. But after thinking about it, I realized that Wayne II was angry with his father for a number of reasons, primarily for what he did to me and for abandoning him like his mother had. However, I knew he still loved him. Wayne II just had to get over the shock and disappointment.

Jane felt hatred for Wayne. I guess hurt is more like it. Jane had always thought of him as a close brother. Jane had loved me so much and witnessed how distraught I'd become, almost to the point of a nervous breakdown, and she resented him. But Jane, being an adult, was able to make polite dinner conversation.

If the boys' non-acknowledgement and Jane's "polite" conversation were my only problems, it wouldn't have been a half-bad Thanksgiving. To add to the fun, over the course of the day, my phone rang exactly forty-two times. The first time I answered it, SHE was on the other line. During the next forty-one times, I just let it ring for I knew who was calling. Oh, she tried desperately! And of course, I couldn't help but answer the phone and listen to what she had to say, and she had plenty to say!

To prove the validity of her statements, she would provide me with very personal family information that only Wayne could have divulged—topics that no one outside the family should have ever been told. The fact that Wayne could so easily provide this woman with such personal information really surprised me. However, I realized it was probably easy for him to do, being drunk and or drugged all the time.

Every time the phone rang, Wayne pleaded with me not to answer it. But I was drawn to that phone, or was it to the person on the other end? Reflecting back on that day, I can't believe how easy it was for me to be "sucked in" by her. For a moment, I had forgotten the conversation that had taken place between her and me. By Wayne returning to me using his free will, her mission had failed and she was defeated! Did he really say those things? Either way, I still distrusted him! Somehow I managed to stop answering the phone, on the forty-third call.

Minus my mother being with us, our daily life settled into a normal routine. Christmas came and went! New Year's came, but we didn't really have the money to do anything special. However, Wayne was called into work to handle an emergency. Considering past events, I should have thought it odd being called into an emergency on New Year's Eve, especially since he worked in pest control.

About two weeks after New Year's, a very familiar voice was on my phone line. It was her! She joyously announced, "Guess where you husband was on New Year's Eve. That's right, he came over to visit me." Even as I'm writing this, over five years later, I can still feel my breath being taken away and an ache throughout my body. "Understand that I have the power to control your husband, and you!" she said. "Could you really stand to lose Wayne? He is too weak of spirit. Wayne is on a self-indulging path, and I'm going to do everything I can to help him fulfill his self-destruction."

Unlike the times before, I didn't listen and hung up quickly! Even though I was shocked, it wasn't as a severe blow as before. I can only assume that part of me didn't believe this whole affair, or should I say possession, would have ended so quickly.

Well, of course, when I confronted Wayne, he denied it. But I didn't believe him. To prove his continued devotion and love for me, Wayne thought it would be a nice idea to renew our marriage vows. Our anniversary was only a few weeks away. So we asked a friend of ours, the priest who had originally married us, to renew our vows.

Wayne went all out! He even rented a luxurious hotel room in Connecticut, which included a built-in spa and Jacuzzi. Even though I had traveled a lot, it was one of the most beautiful rooms I had ever seen. We had even brought a small wedding cake that we ate all alone in the room. I had also brought a beautiful cream-laced dress for the occasion. It was certainly a fantasy weekend in more ways than one.

About two weeks after returning home, Wayne ran into a local grocery store as I sat out in the truck. As I pulled down the passenger's visor mirror to look at my hair, I saw a set of pink lipstick marks imprinted in the mirror. I knew it wasn't my lipstick, because I don't wear make-up. It didn't take me long to realize who the owner of that lipstick was. There was no way out of it this time. Wayne tried to come up with some story about the lipstick being there for awhile, but I wasn't biting.

It was amazing that Wayne could not recognize the fact that this witch was trying desperately to destroy him. Actually, what he didn't realize was that it really had nothing to do with him. She was trying to get to me! As bad as I felt that Wayne was being manipulated by this devil, I had to protect myself and get away from this situation.

Why did Wayne go through this elaborate façade of insisting that we rededicate ourselves to each other when he had no intention of actually committing to me or to our relationship? I didn't know why, but I kept forgetting that there was more than Wayne's will at stake here.

Once again, she called me to gloat. Wayne had actually gone and seen her a day after we returned from our "second honeymoon" trip. I just couldn't believe it. Throughout my life, evil has tried to entice me, scare me, physically hurt me and emotionally cripple me. I wasn't sure how much more I would be able to stand.

Even though I was prepared to walk out of this relationship, I tried pleading with Wayne to listen to me about her. I tried explaining that she was really working through him to get to me, but my words fell on deaf ears.

I had no choice but to shift gears! I decided that I was going to relocate the kids and myself out of state. My company had offered me a job at their corporate office in Minnesota. Although I hated to leave Joe behind with an unstable Jane, I had no recourse. My sanity was quickly fading. I had to leave while I still could.

However, the kids made other plans. Scotty, who was already eighteen, had decided to stay in Rhode Island and move in with several of his friends. I could foresee disaster down the road but, as I had with Wayne, I had to trust that God would see him through.

Wayne II had decided that he also wanted to stay in Rhode Island, but obviously, not with his father. Wayne II had contacted his mother, who agreed that he could live with her. It looked like I would now be alone moving to a strange state. However, the job wouldn't be available for four months. Therefore, I had to try enduring the next four months of constant torment.

This time, Wayne didn't move out. We mutually agreed that we would sell the house, split up our belongings and divorce. Divorce! My Wayne, I never dreamed it would happen. All I could think of was how he initially loved me so deeply, and how it was now all gone.

I tried to distance myself from Wayne during that period. I still begged God to help him break away from this demon, but I had to leave it in God's hands. There was nothing any human being could possibly do. I hoped that if she saw I wasn't interested, she would leave him alone.

It was around the beginning of June, just as I started to prepare for the move to Minnesota, that something strange began happening. Wayne was actually staying at home at night and initiating conversations with me. He spoke to me as he did when we first met. Of course, "she" continued to ring the phone off my wall every night, but this time, neither Wayne nor I were answering her calls.

It was close to the end of June when Wayne made his proclamation that this time; he seriously wanted to try working on our relationship. He asked if he could move to Minnesota with me. My initial thought was "no way." Wayne's antics had turned my heart into stone where he was concerned. Although I didn't think I felt love for him anymore, I did feel compassion for Wayne. He allowed himself to become such an easy target for evil. Most importantly, I wanted to get him away from that devil. I agreed to take him with me. We would see how things went.

I would be lying if I didn't say that it did give me enormous satisfaction when she made one of her infamous phone calls and I was the one who was able to tell her that she had lost. I had never heard such fury in a person's voice. For the remaining two weeks, she went insane calling and riding by our house. But this time, Wayne did not retreat. He continued preparing himself for the move to Minnesota.

Unfortunately, during this two-week period, my sister Mary had to drive up to Rhode Island and pick up Joe. Realizing she was going to have to raise Joe on her own, and not ready to do so, Jane had checked herself into a rehabilitation facility. No one had any idea how long she was going to be there.

So, off Joe went. My heart was broken. After all, Wayne and I had spent so much time raising and nurturing Joe. Wherever Wayne and I went, so did Joe. Joe was also the one that encouraged that Wayne would return. I wanted desperately to take him with me, but we were being put up in a hotel until suitable housing was found. Once we found a house, I figured that we would go and pick up Joe and Jane, depending upon Jane's status.

Either way, I had to witness that puzzled look on his face as Joe waved goodbye. Little did I know at the time that Joe had a horrible adventure awaiting him in the not-too-distance future. A week and a half before we moved, an incident took place during the night, which I wasn't aware of until Wayne brought it to my attention the next morning. Apparently, I was waking up during the night, sitting straight up and pointing to our closet. In a completely jubilant voice I would say, "Look at that bird! Look at that bird!" Wayne went on to say that my eyes were wide open and I never blinked. Of course, Wayne did not see any bird. And for some reason, I couldn't remember anything, which as you know, is so unlike me considering I've been able to reiterate my dreams as a four-year-old in the hospital.

Finally, after a week of this incident occurring each night, something different happened on one particular evening. This time, almost in a transfixed state, I could see the bird! I was aware of what was happening, but could not move. It was a snow-white bird, about two feet tall, with glistening feathers. The bird's feathers were so shiny they were almost blinding. Although the bird did nothing but sit and stare, I felt such sheer joy throughout my body. It was an incredible feeling.

Unfortunately, when Wayne started to talk to me, the bird vanished. I realized that this must have been the bird I was seeing every night but didn't remember. But why had this bird been appearing to me every night for the past week?

As usual, the next morning, after I got out of bed, had my shower, and got dressed, I went over to my jewelry box to look for some earrings. When I pulled open the wooden drawer, there was a necklace lying on top of my earrings. It looked as if it had been carefully placed so that the chain would not get tangled. This was a jewelry box that held only earrings.

As I picked up this necklace, to inspect the ornament attached to the end, I recognized it immediately; it was the "Dove of Peace." Actually, it represented the Holy Spirit. God sends the Holy Spirit with special gifts, such as wisdom, counsel, and prophesy, to name a few.

Besides being amazed that this necklace, which symbolized peace, had come out of nowhere, there was something else I found familiar about it. As I sat at the end of my bed thinking about it, the answer eventually came to me. I thought I recognized the necklace. It was the necklace of my grandmother, who had died approximately four years earlier. It was never given to me, so I'm not sure how it got into my jewelry box. I also realized that the bird I saw perched in the corner of my room all week was that same Dove of Peace/Spirit of God.

And then it all clicked. I took this as a sign from God that peace was headed my way. Even if only for a short time, it was coming. Besides bewilderment, I was now left with a newfound hope and an optimistic attitude. It also made me feel that, as hard as it was going to be leaving Rhode Island, it was something I had to do, at least for now. I also wondered if one of the Holy Spirit's special gifts had been bestowed on me during that week. Actually, I believe that God had already graciously endowed me with these gifts. It was like finding that beautiful rainbow at the end of a terrible storm! Whatever journey God was leading me on, I had to follow. Unfortunately, I was sure that "evil" would be close behind, treading in my footsteps, but I no longer feared it!

The day finally came for the big move. Although assured that I was doing the right thing and that this was all part of God's plan, human feelings such as anger, sorrow and fear now began creeping in. I can't recall a lot of the day. I was in shock, especially when it came time to say goodbye to my kids, not sure when I'd see them again. Within months, my whole family was torn apart! My mother was gone, the kids were gone, and now I was going! The only part of my life that was going with me was the dog.

It wasn't until we got on the road and began driving to Minnesota that my anger intensified. I was angry with Wayne! This was all his fault! I had no desire to ever leave Rhode Island, but now I was leaving, forced to leave! However, I knew I just had to get away from the almost one year of ugliness that had transpired. Although I knew there were extenuating circumstances, I still felt betrayed.

I was also angry that Wayne was so happy. He finally got what he wanted. It was now only him and me, and we were moving so far away. We would be far from our home and families, with virtually no friends except one, our very best friend, Amy. Amy had been very much a part of our lives for years now. I met Amy while on a business trip to Minnesota, my company's corporate headquarters. Amy is a native of Minnesota. She had also spent a lot of time working out of the company's Rhode Island office. That's how we got to know each other so well. That was the one ray of sunshine about moving to Minnesota and that was the opportunity to spend more time with Amy.

The trip to Minnesota would take approximately thirty-two hours by car. The first night, we stayed in a hotel. The next day, we stopped at my brother's house in Chicago to visit. I thought I'd be happy visiting my mother, but I only felt sorrow and animosity toward Wayne. I had allowed myself to be manipulated into getting rid of her. You might well say that devil woman indirectly manipulated me as well as Wayne in some respects! I felt so guilty seeing my mother and having to leave her again. Needless to say, when I finally arrived in Minnesota, I was a mess.

But we acclimated ourselves as best we could to our new surroundings. Wayne tried diligently to make our "aloneness" together just wonderful. Although there were times that I actually experienced some joy, it quickly faded. It wasn't right that my family wasn't with me, and quite frankly, I didn't trust that Wayne would actually stay.

I bought a small townhouse in a suburb of Minneapolis. I liked it because it was close to work and I didn't have to drive on too many strange roads. It was a tri-level house with two huge bedrooms. It was great house for just two people and that's what we were now, just two people, the rest of our family had disappeared.

The big state of Minnesota was a lot different than little Rhode Island. There didn't appear to be any Portuguese or Italians, only German and Swedish people. I felt even more alone. Wayne continued trying to make our time together seem like the honeymoon that we had never got to take. But I was too enraged, too hurt. However, our "honeymoon" was not to last very long! We arrived in the house around the beginning of September. By the end of September, Wayne II was having trouble at his "mother's house."

I had hoped for the best for Wayne II's sake, but anticipated the worst. The problem was that his biological mother never really knew him or understood anything about him. Therefore, she had difficulty relating to his actions and understanding his needs. So, the last weekend in September, Wayne and I got in our truck and headed for Rhode Island to pick up Wayne II.

I can't tell you how secretly thrilled I was to be picking him up. I came into Wayne II's life when he was seven. From that day, I always felt that he was an important part of my life, and now he was coming home to stay. Wayne II adjusted surprisingly well to the Minnesota lifestyle. Even when there was a wind-chill factor of sixty below zero in November, it didn't seem to faze him. I, on the other hand, had a terrible time adjusting. Even though Minnesota was very beautiful and there were a lot of things to do, I longed to go home.

The only reason I got through my time in Minnesota was Amy. Amy was a godsend. She's not really a friend; she is an important part of my family. Amy was the only friend that we spent any time with in Minnesota. Amy spent a lot of time trying to acclimate us to the Minnesota lifestyle. She really helped us to learn our way around. Amy actually made Minnesota both bearable and fun. (Not that Minnesota was bad, it was just too cold, and the culture was so different than what we were use to in Rhode Island.)

As a matter of fact, the day before Thanksgiving, Amy and I went shopping for our Thanksgiving dinner supplies together, and that's when it happened.

12

Jane Defeats the Devil

My sister Mary called to tell me that Jane had gotten out of the rehabilitation facility, picked up Joe three days ago and gone back to Rhode Island on the train. Unfortunately, upon Jane's return to Rhode Island; she went out, supposable for a few hours, and left her new heroine-addict live-in boyfriend to watch Joe.

Well apparently, when she didn't return home that night, with Joe sleeping in the other room, Jane's boyfriend went on a rampage, breaking all the furniture in the house and pulling the phone out of the wall. The boyfriend then took off, leaving Joe alone. He was later found passed out on the ground by the police.

Amazingly, Joe did not wake up until morning. Unfortunately, when Joe did wake up, he found an apartment that was destroyed and discovered that no one was home. Even though he was only four, he tried dialing 911. But the phone didn't work. Not knowing what else to do, Joe went downstairs, sat near the landlord's door and started crying. The landlord found a scared, sobbing Joe and called the police. Mary said that Joe was taken into custody and was going to be placed into a "Children's Center" because he had no relatives in the State of RI. Also, there were no foster homes available that could take him.

After hanging up with Mary, I immediately got on the phone and called the police station that was holding Joe. I explained that although I was out of state, Joe had basically lived with me always, and it had only been a few months that we had been apart. I asked if I could come and pick him up. The police replied that Joe was now a ward of the State of Rhode Island, and unless I was a foster parent, he couldn't be placed with me.

Immediately, I got on the phone with my brother and sister-in-law in Rhode Island (Wayne's relatives), who were foster parents, and asked if they would take Joe temporarily until Wayne and I could get our foster care license. Although already at capacity with the number of children in their household, they agreed to take Joe. It was beneficial for Joe that Wayne and I use to take him to birthday parties for the kids who lived at the house. This was a blessing for Joe that he actually knew the people he was staying with, quite well.

Joe knew my brother and sister-in-law and the kids. Although I felt better that Joe wasn't going to be placed in any "children's center," I felt just heartsick for Joe. He was just a baby, all alone!! Needless to say, it was an awful Thanksgiving, not only for me, but Jane.

Jane had apparently either gotten drunk or high and broke her ankle. She was in the emergency room, and that's why she never came home. However, when the story of the abandonment hit the TV stations and newsstands, Jane was identified at the hospital and, leg cast and all, thrown in jail.

It was Jane that actually called Mary to see if she could go up and get Joe. Jane didn't realize that once the State of Rhode Island had picked up Joe, and that he no longer belonged to her or any of us.

Joe stayed with my in-laws from November until the third week in February. During this time, Wayne and I worked diligently to get our foster care license. We had to meet with a number of social workers, undergo house inspections, and attend classes, the works! Fortunately, during this time, I was able to take two business trips that allowed me to stop over in Rhode Island and visit Joe.

It was so heartbreaking! Each time I would get ready to leave, Joe would beg to go with me! And why wouldn't I take him with me? Didn't I want him either? Joe couldn't understand that it was out of my control. He did understand that he would eventually move to Minnesota with Wayne and me, but he wanted to go now!

Jane had long since got out of jail. During Joe's time in Rhode Island, she was able to have a few scheduled, supervised visitation days with him. Jane was eventually able to make Joe understand that she did not leave him and would have never left him. She just made the mistake of leaving him with a loser, a very costly mistake.

The day finally arrived, and on one snowy day in February, I flew to Rhode Island to take Joe home. I had such mixed emotions. Jane was not allowed to see Joe before he left Rhode Island. All I could think of was her being completely devastated. Really, her primary reason for living was now moving out of state. And even though I got lost driving in a snowstorm that had turned into a furious blizzard, Joe and I still made it to the airport. And even though the airport had cancelled 90% of their flights, our flight wasn't one of them. God had surely meant for us to go home.

When Joe and I arrived home, Wayne's smiling face was waiting for us at the airport. We had turned our office into a bedroom for Joe. It was wonderful to see Joe climbing into his brand new bed with his superhero sheets for the first time. The expression on his face told the story—Joe felt security at last.

Although there were other contributing factors, it was actually this incident that rekindled the joyful relationship that Wayne and I had initially shared. Joe was right. Wayne did come back to us, not only physically but emotionally, and it was Joe's tragedy that help to make it happen. Wayne was given the opportunity to prove that he was the same person I met almost nine years ago.

Well, because Joe was only four years old, I had to find a daycare for him. And because of his experiences, I didn't want him to go to a "facility" daycare.

Once again, right in my path, I came across a daycare provider that was perfect. She provided daycare in a home setting. There were two other boys that were Joe's age. She was also a Christian. It was perfect.

Now our new family started to merge. It went from Wayne and I, just the two of us, to us plus Wayne II and Joe. Eventually, my mother would also move back in with us to assist with Joe. It was fabulous having her back with me! However, even though we got our foster care license, that wasn't the end of the story. Wayne and I had talked with the social worker from Rhode Island regarding the necessary steps that needed to be taken in order to adopt Joe.

Basically, the State of Rhode Island told us that Joe would be eligible for adoption the following May. If Jane contested, the State of Rhode Island would take her to court. The bottom line was that the State of Rhode Island had no plans of ever giving Joe back to Jane. Jane didn't realize this was happening. Jane had high hopes of getting Joe back. I suggested that she move to Minnesota to be closer to Joe. There was nothing keeping her in Rhode Island. Shortly after, Jane did move to Minnesota, just in time to see Joe get on the bus for his first day in kindergarten.

Jane stayed with us for a couple of weeks, then moved into a halfway house. That was the agreement. If Jane was to move to Minnesota, it was with the understanding that she would not be living with us. The courts had instituted a no-contact order. We legally couldn't have Jane stay with us. After the two weeks were up, Amy and I took Jane to the halfway house. Subsequently, Jane still came down to visit Joe whenever possible.

Things seemed to be calming down a bit. I thought it was time to refocus some of my energies. When October rolled around, the Catholic Church that I had joined was looking for Religious Instruction teachers, so I signed up. I had taught a Confirmation program for almost four years, so I felt qualified. I was asked to teach sixth grade. The curriculum was the Old Testament. It sounded challenging, but I decided to give it a try. I found that the sixth grade kids challenging, but, it was good to get back to teaching and have the opportunity to once again spread God's word.

On one particular, unusually snowy, blustery day, I thought for sure class would have been cancelled. Besides the inches of snow rapidly accumulating on previously iced roads, it was also bitter cold, much colder than I had ever experience in Rhode Island. It wasn't until we were in class about twenty minutes that the Religious Education Director decided to dismiss the classes.

After the kids left, I had to stay awhile longer. I had to pack up all of my materials, put the chairs on top of the desks and secure the room. By the time I was ready to leave, all of the teachers had already gone and I was left alone.

As I descended the wide, creaky wooden staircases, I begged God to see me safely home. The impending drive home scared me. When I reached the bottom of the third staircase, I could hear the final echo of the antiquated, wooden side door slam behind me. I started walking toward my car.

I was just ready to put the key into the lock of the driver's side of the door when all of a sudden, I froze. From my currently bent posture, I stood up. With my back facing the church's school, I gradually turned around. To my astonishment, as I gazed up at one of the windows, I saw that the life-sized statue of Our Blessed Lady, which usually stood in the second-floor stairwell facing the descending first-floor stairs, had turned around and was now facing the window, watching me.

Was this my imagination? Our Blessed Lady statue was not facing the window when I left. She was facing the stairs, gazing inside the building, not outside of it! My legs seemed to be moving involuntarily, without my conscious knowledge, closer to the building to get a better look. Sure enough, it was Our Blessed Lady, looking directly at me.

Suddenly, I realized that her magnificent, maternal eyes were protectively watching me. I can't describe the euphoric sensation that was my coursing throughout my body. The fear of driving alone in this treacherous snow had disappeared. I was at peace with the impending drive and did not feel afraid.

After I walked back to my car, opened the door, and got in, I quickly looked in my rearview mirror to find that Our Blessed Lady was still watching me. This time, her arms were now delicately extended. It was almost as if she were embracing me from afar. Before I left, I loudly sang a song of praise in my car and left the parking lot.

I had to make a U-turn in the road that ran parallel to the church. This meant I was to pass by the church again. And as I did, I looked completely to my right to Our Blessed Lady, only to find that she had completely reverted back to her original position. Her back was now facing the window. Our Blessed Lady did what she meant to do, and that was letting me know that I would be all right going home, for she was now personally protecting me. From that day on, whenever I felt alone or afraid, I reflected on that day and remembered that I have a mother in heaven guarding me.

After Thanksgiving and Christmas went by, my major focus needed to shift gears. Joe's year with us was almost completed. A decision regarding Joe's custody had to be made. By January, Jane realized that the State of Rhode Island was not going to place Joe back in her custody. Therefore, Jane did what I considered to be the most courageous act of love that I had ever personally witnessed. To ensure that Joe would remain with a family that loved him and was concerned with his well being, Jane decided to freely allow Wayne and I to adopt Joe.

I know what a heart-wrenching decision this was for Jane. Jane's love for Joe was genuine. Joe was always the most important person in her life. Unfortunately, Jane's health was deteriorating as well. Although Jane had been both alcohol- and drug-free for over half a year at this point, because her body had been so dependant on drugs, she was not able to function without them. Therefore, Jane was placed in a methadone program that left her virtually unable to function on a daily basis.

Most of the time, you would find Jane sleeping in a chair or on the couch. When Jane spoke, her words were always slurred. It was terrible. But we hoped that eventually the medication would be decreased and Jane would gain more control over her life. I assured Jane that even though Joe would be adopted by Wayne and I, she would still be his mother and very much apart of his life.

Although people tried to dissuade me from my decision, claiming that it would be too confusing for Joe, this was a promise I intended on keeping, so the adoption proceedings were initiated. During that time, we also made the decision to move closer to home. We decided that we didn't really want to go back to Rhode Island at this point. We tried thinking of a place that would be, number one, warmer than Minnesota. We also wanted a place that would see us living closer to relatives without being on top of them.

Because we had relatives in Rhode Island, North Carolina, Kentucky and Virginia, we thought it might be nice to live in Virginia. Actually, Virginia was strategically located in conjunction with all the other states that my family resided in. By car, it was approximately nine hours away from Rhode Island and Kentucky. It was six hours away from North Carolina and two hours away from the southern part of Virginia, where my brother lived. Virginia was also a beautiful state and very historical. After reading several books on Virginia, the activities and things to do seemed very family-oriented. So we made our decision, Virginia would be our new home. We began to plan our strategy.

Upon perusing my company's job postings on our Intranet, I found a possible opportunity in Virginia. They were looking for a project manager, a job that fit my qualifications. To my miraculous surprise, I found that the person I would be interviewing with was someone I knew from our sister site in New England. The interview went exceptionally well and I was hired in April of 1997.

Joe's adoption court date was scheduled for May 13, 1997. On May 12, Joe, Wayne, Jane and I flew to Rhode Island. As I watched Jane on the plane, I could see apprehension and grief written all over her face. Jane was concerned that Joe would not understand that she was not "giving him away." If the State of Rhode Island would have allowed it, and her health wasn't poor, she would have continued trying to raise him.

Needless to say, May 13 was full of mixed emotions. I was amazed at the cruelty and insensitive way at which the State of Rhode Island handled this matter. They were fully aware of what I considered to be a sensitive situation. Specially, Wayne and I were adopting Joe to secure his future within our family. Jane did not want to let him go but knew that she was too sick from both drug abuse and HIV to appropriately care for him. Unlike some adoptions, Jane was not being completely removed from his life. My goal was to ensure that she spent as much time with him as possible during her remaining time. I felt it would be both good for Joe and Jane. So in one room, Jane sat alone, reluctantly signing away her child, while just next door, the judge was happily announcing that Wayne and I were officially Joe's parents. Then we all had to stand there smiling while the court stenographer took a picture of us with the judge. As we stepped out of the judge's chambers, there was Jane, sitting alone silently, in an empty row of chairs.

There was a deafening silence on the ride back to Scotty's apartment. (That's where Jane was staying.) Jane was both shocked and bewildered! Certainly, if we suffer for any of our crimes here on earth, Jane would have been given credit for this event. It probably had to be one of the saddest times Jane had ever experienced, and unfortunately, she had to go through it alone. However, I was determined to make Joe still very much apart of her life.

We arrived back in Minnesota, and it was time to prepare for the big move. I had to wind down things at work, the house had to be sold, and we had to find a new house in Virginia. There were a million things to do in a short period of time. We had to be in Virginia by the second week in June. Maybe the move to Virginia would be a nice diversion for Jane, for she, naturally, was going with us.

Amazingly enough, within a four-week period of time, we were ready to depart. During that time, Wayne, Joe and I had taken a trip to Virginia to find our new house. We didn't have much luck. As a result, we moved into an apartment, which would be alright for now. My company was good about selecting a nice apartment for people who were relocating.

As I sat on that plane heading to our new home I couldn't help but think how much had happened to me in three years. I went through a year of my husband cheating on me, leaving Rhode Island, living in Minnesota and now moving to Virginia. I know that military families experience this all the time, but I was not from a military family. I felt so displaced. However, this time I welcomed the move. I looked forward to moving to Virginia.

As we first settled in, I was in awe over the lower food prices, car insurance, everything. The scenery and weather were just beautiful. Upon our arrival, we had to hunt for two things. The first was a house. And within a two-week period, we decided to purchase a new house and have it built.

It was to be located in one of those "housing communities." At that time, Rhode Island had nothing comparable, so I didn't know what to expect. I wish I had known. The second thing we had to find was a place for Jane to go to get her methadone. Eventually, we did find the place and naturally, it was in the trashy part of downtown Richmond. Jane was no longer able to drive, so Wayne and I would have to take her each day for her methadone.

Unfortunately, it was the same thing everyday: she would come home and fall asleep, sometimes while she was talking. The times that she was awake were becoming less frequent. The numerous doctors Jane had seen from Minnesota, and now Virginia, said that she would never be able to go off of the medication. Her body had been on drugs so many years that it would not be possible to be medication free.

It was now July and the summer was really kicking in. There is a huge difference between Julys in Minnesota verses Julys in Virginia. Jane seemed to actually be doing a little better in the month of July. Our apartment complex had a pool and Jane took advantage by taking Joe as much as possible. They played games together, read stories, watched movies, and had fun. It was actually the most time Jane had ever spent with Joe. It was wonderful for her and Joe.

I was becoming extremely busy with my new job as well as the planning details of a new house. However, the house wouldn't actually be ready until November. Sometime around the end of July, Jane started apartment hunting. By the 6th of August, Jane had found an apartment, one that her disability money could afford.

Jane would now be renting the downstairs of a house. The landscape surrounding the house and the entire neighborhood was magnificent. There were all types of trees, flowers and bushes. It was simply beautiful. Jane was so excited about the new apartment. She and I went shopping for new things for the apartment: plates, a toaster, an ironing board, a small kitchen table and chairs.

Jane had either lost or sold her personal belongings, so, except for a few remembrances, everything was brand new. It was as if Jane's new things symbolized her new illegal drug-free life. Unfortunately, the doctors told her that she would always be required to take methadone. If she didn't, her body would not be able to take the shock and simply shut done. Once Jane got settled into her new place, we decided to allow Joe to visit one day over the weekend, and then to gradually allow him to spend the night. Jane had proven that she was now responsible enough to spend more time with Joe.

Jane wanted all of us to visit the first weekend she was in her new apartment. Unfortunately, I wouldn't be able to go up to visit until the next weekend, because I was leaving for a business trip on Sunday. I told Jane that I would see her next weekend, but I could tell by her voice that she had hoped that we could visit sooner. However, as planned, I did leave for my business trip on Sunday. I was to attend a week-long ongoing training session.

It was after class on a Tuesday night that I called home to see how things were going. My mother's voice was obviously shaky and upset. She informed me that Jane was in the hospital. Jane had told my mother that there was something wrong with her pancreas and that she was in a lot of pain. My mother said she had moaned and cried throughout the conversation. My mother gave me the hospital's phone number and I immediately called.

After being transferred between a few nurses, I was connected with her doctor. Thinking that this was a secondary illness as a result of her being HIV positive, before allowing the doctor to speak, I asked if this problem with her pancreas was life threatening.

He said to me, "No, it isn't life threatening, but by the time this episode subsides, your sister will wish she were dead!" I was totally confused! The doctor then explained to me that Jane had been brought in by rescue the night before. Apparently, she went out on a drinking binge and developed pains that were so severe, she collapsed to the ground.

Once the doctor assured me she would be all right in a few days. I had mixed emotions of anger, frustration and disappointment. Jane had done so well! She had been illegal drug- and alcohol-free for so long! What happened? Then I realized Jane was probably not use to being truly alone. Or maybe, really missing Joe, she sought out the only comfort familiar to her.

When I called Jane, she sounded awful. She was gasping for breath and moaning with every word she spoke. As I listened to Jane crying about what she had done,

I felt my usual empathy for her. I tried to reassure her that Joe and I were still going to be very much apart of her life. Sounding very much out of breath, I told Jane that I would call her tomorrow. I ended the call by reassuring her that I would never give up on her, and that I loved her.

Well, it was Wednesday and another day of class went by. Before leaving work, I decided to call Jane to see how she was doing. However, when I called her room number, no one answered. I assumed Jane was sleeping. So I called the nurse's station on her floor to see how she was doing.

When I explained to the nurse that I was Jane's sister, her silence seem to last an eternity. The nurse finally spoke and said, "We've tried to reach you or someone in your family all day. Around 11:00 a.m., Jane lapsed into a coma and is in intensive care. I'm afraid she's not doing well. Why don't you wait while I get the doctor for you."

As I felt myself stop breathing, I started questioning what I had heard. And as minutes went by, while waiting for the doctor, I managed to convince myself that I hadn't understood the nurse and would wait for the doctor to talk to me. As the doctor got on the phone, almost verbatim, he repeated what the nurse had said, "Unexpectedly, Jane lapsed into the coma around 11:00 and is intensive care." The doctor elaborated, "Unfortunately, Jane's organs are starting to shut down, and she's not going to make it."

Now, completely not allowing myself to comprehend his words, I could only repeat the word "what?" over and over. As the doctor's words finally began making sense, the only question I could ask was, "Should I have my brothers and sister fly in to see Jane?"

It wasn't until the doctor said "only if they hurry," that the reality of the situation became clear. This doctor was telling me that Jane was going to die! Somehow, my now stiffened hand managed to remove the phone receiver from my ear and instinctively place it back down. Every muscle in my body had completely tensed up.

Almost blindly, I managed to walk back to Amy's desk. In a calm, almost eerie voice I said, "Amy, the doctor just told me that Jane is going to die!" Now in a state of panic, I didn't know how to do, what to say, my thoughts became completely jumbled. Amy immediately grabbed both our pocketbooks and escorted me out of the building. As I walked, my eyes remained fixed, almost as if they had forgotten how to blink.

Then it happened! It was almost as if I had just awoken from a trance and realized Jane was going to die. I exploded into a shrill, almost deafening cry. I started screaming for God to help me. I begged for Jane not to die, please God, you can do anything, don't let this happen. Don't let Jane die!!!

When I arrived at Amy's house, I spoke to Wayne, who, although very empathetic over Jane, seemed more concerned over me. Wayne agreed to take my mother to the hospital immediately. I then called Jack, Mary and Ted. Each one of them, sounding as grief-stricken as myself, were now making plans to arrive in Virginia, praying that they would get to speak to Jane before it was too late.

Unfortunately, I wasn't able to get a flight out until the next day. But fortunately, I would spend that long, horrible night with Amy. I don't know what I would have ever done without Amy; she stayed diligently by my side throughout the entire night. It was a little after midnight when the phone rang. As Amy went to answer it, I could feel my heart almost bursting through my chest. I knew this call was about Jane.

Amy sorrowfully handed me the phone and I knew what I was going to hear. It was Wayne on the phone, informing me that Jane had just died. Intense emotions consumed my body, and I could barely stand. As Amy helped me to the couch, I realized that it was over. Jane's life was over, but so was her agony. However, at that very moment, it wasn't much of a comfort to me.

Needless to say, I was up the rest of the night. Besides being so unhappy about Jane, I was also fearful! Fearful that Jane would appear to me. I didn't know why I was so afraid. I think it's because I wasn't sure what had happened to Jane.

Although Jane was really a good-hearted, caring and compassionate person, she had done a lot of evil things throughout her life. Yes, I'm sure she was manipulated by the devil, but nonetheless, they were evil deeds. Also, knowing my history, I was sure I was going to see her. Miraculously, I didn't. In my fragile state, I probably would have had a heart attack. It's amazing though. Less than a year later, I longed for just one opportunity to see Jane again. Where did Jane go? Would I ever see her again?

The morning finally came. I somehow managed to get on the plane and even make my connections. However, I would not allow myself to think of Jane while I was on the plane. I was able put up a complete wall. When I stepped off the plane, Wayne, my sister Mary and brother Ted were awaiting my arrival. Needless to say, seeing all those people who knew and loved Jane as I did immediately prompted a very emotional reunion. My brother Jack had driven in from Virginia.

To my surprise, Joe had not been told of Jane's death. Wayne and I had the sad responsibility of informing Joe. Although he knew that Wayne and I had adopted him, after he stopped crying, the first words he spoke were, "My brother is dead, my mother is dead, and now I'm all alone." It was so heartbreaking. We had to immediately assure Joe that he was not "all alone" and that he had an entire family that loves him.

Unfortunately, practical matters needed attention. Funeral arrangements would have to be made. Jane's apartment needed to be cleaned out. There were things to do. With no insurance or money, funeral arrangements were not going to be easy. As soon as I arrived at the apartment from the airport, I called the State of Virginia's welfare office to see what could be done. They offered $500 dollars for a cremation. Although I found a wonderful funeral home, this would still not be enough. Fortunately, our very generous cousin, Sharon, sent a substantial donation toward Jane's expenses, which would cover the remaining costs.

I put the money I had toward special Gregorian masses that Catholics believe will ensure Jane's soul not be commended to hell and that she would ultimately make it to heaven. We also had to get in touch with a priest and schedule a mass. All the arrangements were made. Jane was to be cremated the next day.

It wasn't until three years later that I would be told what occurred the night before Jane was cremated. As I mentioned, my brother Jack drove in from another part of Virginia for the funeral. During the night, Jack was awoken by the sound of crying from a bedroom. Again, we were in a small apartment, still waiting for our house to be built. Jack had been sleeping out in the living room. There were three bedrooms. My mother and Mary were in one, Wayne and I were in the other and Wayne II and Joe were in the third one. Jack walked over to the closest bedroom, which was Joe's bedroom. Through the closed door, Jack could hear the crying sounds from this bedroom. Assuming that it was Joe, Jack went inside to comfort him. However, when Jack opened the door, to his astonishment, Joe was sound asleep. As he looked to the right of the room, he saw Jane sitting in my mother's rocking chair. Jane never acknowledged Jack. She just simply stared at Joe and sorrowfully, quietly continued to cry. Jane never got up or approached Joe. However, she was holding and hugging his favorite Humpty Dumpy stuffed animal in her hands.

Oddly, even though my brother Ted was in the living room, he never heard the crying. Then again, Jack is the one with the gift. The story holds up because only Wayne, I and my mother knew that the Humpty Dumpy stuffed animal was Joe's favorite. Being in the Navy and out to sea all the time, Jack didn't really know Joe. Therefore, seeing Jane holding this stuffed animal had to be real.

The next day came. Jane was cremated and laid to rest beside her son Michael in North Carolina. It was done! Now was the real time to grieve, and though I did (and still do every day), a profound thought hit me. The sequence of events had come full circle.

As a result of Jane's life with drugs and alcohol, she had lost her son. However, fortunately, Joe was placed in a foster home of loving and familiar faces. Because of this tragedy, Jane stopped drinking and using drugs. Discovering that the State of Rhode Island had no plans of ever giving Joe back, Jane made the most unselfish decision of her life—she gave up Joe for adoption. And being a true mother at heart, Jane ensured that Joe was placed in a loving and stable home.

I believe when Jane went on that drunken binge that fateful night, God simply called it a day!

Jane had managed to redeem herself with the sacrifices made throughout the year. Jane's life mission was over. For had Jane continued, in her "soul destructive" ways, she might have ended up back in the grips of the devil. Ironically, death was Jane's salvation. Jane had defeated the devil! God had once again proven himself to be a merciful, loving God for who else could have carefully planned the events that successfully lead to both Joe and Jane's salvation. As I ran the sequence of events over and over in my mind, I realized how masterfully and meticulously each event unfolded. However, most importantly, our family had proven victorious over the devil and his evil works.

The first Christmas after Jane's death had finally arrived. Besides knowing that Jane would not be here, I had to look at Christmas mementos that she had given to me. It was terrible! The worst part would be going to church. I already anticipated a very emotional scene. As I sat in the back of that church during midnight mass, I could feel my heart racing and my eyes welling up with tears. I tried hiding myself by putting my head down. I dared not look up.

Suddenly, as if someone had whispered in my ear to raise my head and see, I found myself looking forward. To my utter wonder and astonishment, to the right of the altar stood an angel near the tabernacle.

Apparently, I was the only one to see the angel, for no one else was making a commotion. His profile was facing right. The angel was approximately seven feet tall, if not taller, with shoulder-length sandy hair, dressed in a white garment, holding a candle with both of his hands. The angel stood stern and still, and seemed to be guarding the tabernacle. The angel never turned his head or moved at all. His eyes were fixed on the tabernacle that housed the body of Christ.

Throughout the mass, the angel made no movements or facial gestures. He stood at that tabernacle until communion was given out. Then the angel disappeared. While contemplating why I had seen this angel while I was so deep in thought about Jane, it came to me. This was the day of our Savior's birth. That angel was guarding the living body and blood of Christ. And with this body and blood of Christ, we will all have life after dead, including Jane. I believe that God was telling me that day that Jane would be reborn into everlasting life someday. Although I was still in such pain over Jane's death, I was at peace. For I was given the greatest Christmas present of all—hope!

I would find that other such signs of hope and God's love would continue to present themselves over the years. Unknown to me, these other signs of Jane's spirit "living on" would soon be revealed.

13

Chicago—Dimensions Collide

After two Christmas seasons had passed and the Easter season was just around the corner, my traveling for work had doubled. After Jane died, I decided to apply for a training job within my company. Jane's death made me realize how unexpectedly short life can be. Therefore, I decided to work in a field that always interested me, teaching.

With my company's organization, trainers/teachers always received a lower salary than most of the other positions and were viewed as "important employees." However, in my earlier days with the company, training always made me feel as if I was assisting my fellow co-workers in helping them to retain their jobs, their livelihood. I was always genuinely interested in their welfare, but at the same time, after training sessions, I was usually left with feelings of self-fulfillment, gratification and more importantly, being needed.

However, I didn't expect to be traveling so excessively. During this time in my life, traveling was a good thing, at least for me. I was so busy preparing for travel that I didn't have time to think of anything else. Well, except Jane—that would never end.

In the month of April, I was scheduled to conduct a training session for our Chicago office. As usual, I was flying alone. If anything, I was certainly getting to know myself. This was something I had been never able to do my whole life. It had always been so filled with others and their needs that I never really paid attention to myself.

When I arrived in Chicago, I found that I had been reserved into a historically-preserved hotel from the 1920s. It was simply gorgeous. Both the outside and inside of the building reflected the architecture and style of that era. When I opened the door to my room, it consisted of the same 1920s motif. Everything from the pictures to the furniture and lighting were indicative of that period. The television and cable were the only reminders that I was actually living in the 1990s.

Although the room's ambiance was charming and very elegant, almost immediately, there was something that didn't seem right. Now, by this time in my career, I had been traveling almost thirteen years for this company, and needless to say, I had stayed in a lot of hotel rooms. In all those years, I never felt uncomfortable about any of the rooms, maybe it was because of the old, preserved look of the hotel. It wasn't until I was ironing my clothes for work the next day and I saw multiple human shadows against the wall that I became a tad concerned, especially since I was the only person in the room.

It only got worse when I tried turning the knob to the closet door so that I could hang my clothes up and it wouldn't turn. As hard as I tried, it wouldn't open. When I finally gave up and hung my outfit on the towel rack in the bathroom, I heard the soft creaking of the closet door as it slowly opened by itself. Somehow, I managed to convince myself that the room was just settling because it was old.

After I came back from dinner, got in my pajamas, jumped into bed and started watching one of my favorite 1960s comedies, I forgot that the early evening events had even occurred. However, at approximately 10:48, as I lay there continuing to watch television, There was a sound as though someone was trying to open my hotel room door.

Now, this had happened to me once or twice during my traveling days. It was always someone who had the wrong room. Either the hotel had given them the wrong room key or they were trying the wrong door. As I tried to get out of bed to see who was at the door, I found myself completely paralyzed. I knew I wasn't sleeping for I could still hear and see the television show and everything around me. I was able to follow the conversations that were taking place in the show and hear every word. I just couldn't move.

As my eyes and ears remained fixed on the door, I could hear someone using a key to get in, but how could this be? The door did not have a keyhole to place a key in. Although the hotel's theme was based on a 1920s style, the doors were all equipped with swipe-card door locks. Nevertheless, someone was getting into this room with a key.

As the door nonchalantly opened, a man with a tan top hat, trench coat and briefcase came strolling in. Although I was in complete shock and horror, I couldn't scream, I couldn't even blink. The man placed his briefcase on the table and took off his hat. As I lay there stunned, watching the man, I realized something. This man wasn't aware that I was even in the bed. Why didn't he notice me? The bed could immediately be seen upon entry. It was almost as if we were living in two different dimensions. However, that didn't make me feel any better.

As the man proceeded to loosen his tie and take off his suit jacket, I feverishly tried screaming and getting my body to move away so that I could flee from this man. He then proceeded to remove his shirt and pants, leaving only his boxer shorts and socks on. As he approached the bed, I thought I was going to have a heart attack. I had never been so frightened in my life.

He proceeded to push back the covers, climb into the empty side of the bed, and roll over as if he was going to sleep. He was still completely oblivious to the fact that I even existed. As I lay there stunned and shocked, the man continued silently sleeping. However, maybe after fifteen minutes, the man suddenly disappeared. And as he did, I was able to gain control over my body again. Horrified, I began to think, did the man disappear or did I simply return to the correct dimension?

Was this man just returning back to this hotel room, and if so, why this many years later? Did he die in this room? If not, did I somehow get caught in an event that had happened in this man's life? He had to have been dead by now. He appeared to be in his middle to late forties. And based on his clothing, I would judge this event had taken place sometime in the 1950s.

Although it didn't feel like the out-of-body-experience I had when Scotty was a baby, the dynamics were similar. Unlike the first experience, I was aware of what was happening as well as the spirits that tormented me. I was also able to leave and return to my body.

I am not a psychic, nor a parapsychologist, nor have I ever talked to either of the two. I can only explain to you the way these occurrences felt to me in layman's terms. Never having even read a scary book or seen a horror movie, I have nothing on which to base these experiences. My real-life experiences were always about as much as I could handle.

Maybe an expert could more correctly analyze this event. However, unlike any of those "supposed" experts who try explaining supernatural events as scientific realities, I actually lived this experience. After this particular event, I would find myself seeing other entities outside the realm of human reality. Not only was I experiencing these phenomena, but now Wayne was as well.

Wayne had never been much for religion or believing in ghosts, devils or witches. That is, until he met me. But it wasn't until years later. Whenever I told Wayne one of my supernatural stories, he would just laugh and attribute it to an overactive imagination. It wasn't until that trip to Chicago that Wayne experienced his own "next-world" experience.

I didn't tell Wayne what had happened to me in Chicago, fearing that he would have thought I was really going crazy. I don't know if it was because of his exposure to me or because he had experienced firsthand the powers of good and evil, but whatever the reason, Wayne was now being visited himself.

I shouldn't use the word "visit." Actually, these ghostly apparitions would physically "attack" Wayne whenever I was away. The second night I was away, Wayne had just gotten into bed and turned off the lights. Wayne sleeps on the left side of the bed, away from the bedroom door, near the window.

Wayne has difficulty sleeping whenever I'm away, so he had already lain there a few minutes, making an effort to settle himself in. About a half-hour went by when Wayne felt a strange "presence" that seemed to be moving around his head, over his chest and through the space between his back and the bed.

After fumbling a few minutes with the lamp switch, he turned on the small table lamp next to his bed. However, he didn't see anything. At the time, Wayne was certainly not afraid of anything and didn't give the possibility of spirits a second thought. But nonetheless, he couldn't explain the strange feelings that surrounded his body.

Was it some type of insect gnawing at him? No, Wayne thought, the body mass of whatever this was too large to be a bug. But it was now getting late and Wayne knew that he needed to get some sleep in order to face the next grueling workday. Once again, minutes passed and the floating presence returned.

Although diminished, Wayne could still see the entire bedroom thanks to the nightlight near his bedside. Lying on his right side, Wayne could see the bedroom door, our master bathroom and my side of the bed. There was no sign of anyone or anything. Wayne then turned on his left side to survey the other half of the room, when standing silently by his bedside were three Black Mist Men.

Wayne was stunned. It was the first time he felt completely horrified! Wayne described these three Black Mist Men as ranging from 4'9" to 5'10" in height. They consisted of mist with no substance. They had no visible facial features or extremities.

However, within seconds after Wayne noticed them, they began striking him. They punched his face and body. As Wayne jumped out of bed, they continued beating his face and body. In a rapidly-paced, circular motion, the three Black Mist Men continued to surround Wayne.

Wayne didn't know what they were beating him with, since they had no visible hands or feet. Wayne continued to forge ahead toward the door, but could only make small strides. It was when Wayne reached my bureau and placed his hands on my statue of Jesus, Mary and Joseph that the three Black Mist Men retreated. They didn't disappear. They just retreated toward the window.

Wayne said that he remembered my mother telling him to use holy water to protect him against evil, so he quickly grabbed my plastic Blessed Mary holy-water bottle off the bureau and unscrewed the cap, which was in the shape of a crown. Wayne quickly blessed himself with the water and after doing so, poured the remaining holy water into his hands. A second later, he flung the holy water at the entities, and they immediately dissolved. With his heart fiercely pounding, Wayne sat on that floor, clutching the statue for the remainder of the night. The next night, although he feared the three Black Mist Men would return, they did not. Wayne chose not to tell me this story until I returned home from my trip to Chicago. Little did he know I'd have a surprise story for him as well.

What makes this so eerie to me is that I had never told Wayne about my experience with the Black Cloud Mist Man.

Unfortunately, that would not be the last time these three Black Mist Men entities visited Wayne. Subsequently, every time I was on a trip, at least one of the nights, the three Black Mist Men would appear to Wayne. As they had the time before, these entities would start beating Wayne while he was in bed. However, it got shorter each time they appeared. Wayne tried fighting back but was unsuccessful. It wasn't until he blessed himself with holy water that they would disappear or move farther away.

Why didn't these entities appear while I was in the room? For some reason, did they fear me, and if so, was it because I possessed powers? What kinds of powers did I possess? Good, evil or both? Although I like to think that I have led a halfway decent life, it wasn't always righteous! Why would these entities fear me? Maybe they didn't fear me at all, maybe they were simply instructed to leave me alone.

What even makes this situation more bizarre is that these entities only visited Wayne when I was away. Although I had seen the Black Cloud Mist Man, I myself had never seen these particular entities before. I finally decided to talk to my mother about the apparitions that were assaulting Wayne in the night.

Although Wayne went to confession on a regular basis, my mother suggested that he not confess all of his sins to the priest. Therefore, evil was able to torture him because of his unclean soul. By confessing to the priest, in the name of God, these sins would be forgiven and evil spirits would no longer have any hold on Wayne. Wayne promptly rectified that situation the following weekend by confessing his unspoken sins.

Once again, I had to travel on business the following Monday.

Tuesday night when I made my usual nightly call, Wayne told me that he was still being haunted. However, this time it was different. Instead of three Black Mist Men appearing, there was only one. Instead of the Black Cloud Mist Man pouncing all over Wayne, he stood both silent and motionless by Wayne's bedside. It was only minutes before the spirit disappeared.

Why did only one spirit appear? Had Wayne not completely purged all of his sins to the priest, or was this entity commanded to stay behind as a symbol that evil was not about to let Wayne's soul go so easily without a fight? While Wayne was experiencing horrible apparitions, I was also shockingly surprised one evening.

It was several weeks before Easter. I was sleeping with my back turned toward Wayne and my head facing the door, when I was awoken by a strange sensation that someone or something was lying next to me on my left-hand side. Even though I knew that Wayne was beside me, it felt like there were more than two of us in the bed. Throughout the years, having had numerous children sleep with us, for one reason or another, I knew what it felt having three or more people crunched into a queen-size bed.

As I cautiously turned around, sitting straight up, there appeared to be a woman of sorts who measured over six feet. She wasn't actually in the bed, just resting on top of the comforter. Tall and slender in stature, she was exquisite. Her clothes were a dazzling white. It was difficult for me to see her face because of her height. But she sat perfectly straight and erect. Her face was pointed straight up, in the direction of heaven.

Within seconds, this woman, or angel, started singing in the highest, perfectly-pitched soprano voice I had ever heard! It was so loud it was deafening. However, the words that came out of her mouth were foreign. They were not words from another country, but words from another world. As she continued singing, she lifted her hands and arms to the sky. It was then I realized that she was glorifying God.

I couldn't understand why my family wasn't running into the bedroom to see where the noise was coming from. Even more peculiar was why Wayne didn't wake up. Although beautiful, her voice was so shrill; it could have truly awakened the dead. I was both in awe and terrified.

As my arms and hands cautiously extended behind her back, I started forcefully shaking Wayne to wake him up. However, no matter how hard I tried, Wayne would not wake up. I soon realized that for some reason, he wasn't meant to wake up. Apparently, I was unable to see Wayne's visitors and he was unable to see mine.

I know you might be thinking that the reason neither one of us ever saw the other's spirits were because they were only parts of dreams. However, in this case I found out later that Wayne could hear the singing and feel me shaking him—he just couldn't open his eyes. Wayne swears that he was fully awake. However, he was unable to respond.

It wasn't until the woman disappeared that Wayne was able to open his eyes. That was a confirmation to me that I was not dreaming. Throughout my life and experiences, I have always been able to decipher dreams from reality. Remember that I've already had dreams that came true as well. It wasn't until several months later, still thinking about the incident, that I remembered Mrs. Hanson.

That entity was singing the same song Mrs. Hanson had sung the night I saw her rocking her baby in the chair. I had never heard the song before, or the melody.

It wasn't until this singing entity sang her song that I was able correlate it back to the song Mrs. Hanson had sung.

For all these years I thought Mrs. Hanson was singing to her baby, when in fact, she was probably singing to God.

14

Special Gifts for the Next Generation

Well, our ghostly visitors weren't the only surprises Wayne and I encountered in 1998. That January, our son Scotty also decided to move to Virginia to pursue his education. But he didn't come alone; his girlfriend Chloe came as well. Just in case you've lost count, now living with us was Joe, Wayne II, Chloe, Scotty and my mother. Thank God it was a big house

By May, Scotty had broken up with Chloe, who ended up moving out. That July, Scotty found out that he was going to be a father. No, Chloe was not the girlfriend who was pregnant. A former girlfriend, who was still living in Rhode Island, was pregnant. Apparently, Scotty was the only guy she was seeing when she got pregnant.

We found out that the baby was going to be a girl. Although Scotty was no longer seeing this girl, he still wanted very much to be part of the baby's life, emotionally and financially. Wayne and I ended up taking a trip to Rhode Island to meet the mother of our future first grandchild.

Olivia (the baby's mother) seemed like a very levelheaded girl who had career direction and motivation in her life. Unfortunately, there was one serious problem; she was still in love with Scotty. But Scotty was a man on the prowl. Now that he had broken up with Chloe, he was living the bachelor life.

Olivia, Wayne and I agreed that no matter how the situation unfolded, our granddaughter would be not caught in the middle. To this day, I have found Olivia to be a woman true to her word. During August of that year, our beautiful granddaughter, Felicity, was born. Needless to say, we were just thrilled. Olivia and Felicity came up in October to visit with us. Felicity was just beautiful. She had the sweetest face and, surprisingly, my large green eyes. Her skin was fair and she had luxuriant reddish-blond hair.

As I admired Felicity, I couldn't help but wonder if she would possess the family gifts of prophesy and vision of the spiritual world—only time would tell. I wasn't sure if I would ever really know. I decided not to share these stories with Olivia. I wasn't really sure how she would respond.

After only a short visit, Olivia and Felicity returned back home to Rhode Island. Wayne and I had decided that we would try to get out to Rhode Island at least once every three months.

Shortly after their visit, the holiday season was upon us. It was Thanksgiving, and my brother Ted, with his wife and children, came for dinner as usual. What I didn't realize was how unusual this Thanksgiving would turn out to be.

As always, my Thanksgiving dinner consisted of a ridiculous amount of food. But loving to cook as I do, this was common for our family. In following with tradition, the day after Thanksgiving, we kicked off the Christmas season by visiting the shopping mall. After shopping in the only two malls located in this section of Virginia, we decided to hit one of the department stores in search of sales.

As Wayne and I headed toward the department store's entrance, Ted, my mother, Joe and Ted's family were just getting out of their car. Wayne and I decided to proceed into the store without them. Upon entering the store, I saw something that was so shocking and upsetting that my brain couldn't immediate comprehend what was happening. Once my eyes were able to clearly focus again, I saw Chloe, Scotty's former girlfriend, looking like she was about eight months pregnant.

Wayne almost simultaneously noticed Chloe as well. Wayne immediately bent down and whispered in my ear, "Let's go the other way!" Trust me; it was also the first thought that came into my mind as well. But if she was pregnant with Scotty's child, I wanted to know.

Still retaining my bold New England traits, I walked up to Chloe and said, "Hi, asked her if she had a nice Thanksgiving, and then asked her if Scotty was the father of her baby."

Chloe said, "Yes."

I soon discovered that Scotty had known ever since May that Chloe was pregnant! He knew even before he found out about Olivia being pregnant! Chloe said that Scotty was too afraid to tell us. What she didn't realize was why Scotty was too afraid to tell us.

Anyway, Chloe told us that she was going to have a girl. She was due in January. All I could think of were these two sisters, who were going to be maybe four or five months apart! I asked her when she last saw Scotty, and she said, just the other day. Scotty had been seeing her all along and didn't tell us.

I didn't always have to see the devil in a dream or reality to experience his evil powers. Here was my son, who was about to have two daughters from two different women, and not married to either one of them.

When I told Chloe about Olivia's baby, she was shocked. She did say that she had heard rumors, but Scotty tried convincing her they weren't true, and of course, she wanted to believe him. At the end of our conversation, Chloe agreed to stay in touch and stop by the house next week.

When Wayne and I picked up Scotty after work, I sarcastically said to him, "A strange thing happened to me today. I was out shopping for one granddaughter when I found out I really should have been shopping for two." I thought I was going to surprise him, but he was already made aware of the fact that I knew about the baby. Chloe had called him.

Chloe ended up spending the Christmas holiday and weekend with us. During the week that followed Christmas, Chloe had a doctor's appointment and it was suggested that she be induced to have the baby.

It was decided that Chloe would go in on December 31, New Year's Eve, to have our newest grandchild. So on December 31, our Eliza Jane was born. Eliza Jane's birth weight was the same as Scotty's birthday, 7-14. In some way, I believe there's a connection here.

Chloe was also kind enough to take my sister Jane's middle name for the baby. Eliza Jane was absolutely gorgeous. Unlike her sister, Felicity, Eliza Jane had the Portuguese olive complexion, with silky raven-black hair and big blue eyes, like Scotty. However, Eliza Jane's eyes later turned into a lovely hazel green. I found it odd that both my granddaughters had basically the same shape and color of my eyes.

Special Gifts for the Next Generation   119

I remember reading an old expression once: "The eyes are the window to the soul." With both granddaughters having my eyes, I couldn't help but wonder if they would also share some of my other traits.

While Felicity grew to look more like her English, Scottish and Irish ancestors, Eliza Jane had much more of a Portuguese look. Although both girls are beautiful, Eliza Jane is much more mysterious. Unfortunately, because Felicity lived in Rhode Island, I was only able to spend a minimal amount of time with her. Wayne and I usually took at least four long-weekend trips a year to Rhode Island.

Even if only for a day, we would always spend time with Felicity. At two years old, Felicity was a cheerful baby who was always smiling. She seemed to take to everyone so easily. She was also very adventurous and bright.

As for Eliza Jane, besides her mysterious features, the events surrounding her day of birth were very peculiar. Prior to Eliza Jane being born, Chloe was abruptly forced to move from an apartment she had been sharing with a friend. Her friend was getting married and couldn't have Chloe as a roommate any longer.

Oddly, there was this older woman that Chloe had worked who, upon hearing of Chloe's dilemma, had offered her to move into her home. This woman and her husband happened to have two extra bedrooms in their home that they were willing to rent to Chloe.

When Chloe explained the situation to me when we first saw each other Thanksgiving Day in the department store, I thought it was strange, but didn't really say anything at that time. After all, this woman didn't really even know Chloe.

Before Chloe was induced on December 31st, she had asked Scotty to assist with the baby's birth. Through the last three months of Chloe's pregnancy, she and Scotty seemed to have grown closer. Naturally Scotty wanted to be there for the birth of his child. Because Scotty was not driving at the time (his license was temporarily taken away for drunk driving) he asked if I would take him to the hospital. Chloe had already invited me to the hospital, so I was more than willing to assist.

When I arrived at the hospital, Chloe was already in the labor room, and to my surprise, the woman was with her. Originally, I thought this woman was only staying with Chloe until we arrived, but she made her real intentions of staying perfectly clear. This woman planned on staying until Chloe had the baby. She even brought the outfit that SHE had picked out for the baby to go home in. It was apparent that something wasn't right with this situation. She gave herself too much control of this event. Although my initial intentions were to drop Scotty off and have him call me when the baby was born, in light of the situation, I decided to stay.

Who was this woman? As the hours progressed, this woman's manipulation tactics became all too clear. She was not only trying to take over the situation, but Chloe and Eliza Jane as well. Through the course of numerous discussions, I found out that her own four children wanted nothing to do with her. I assumed it was because of her possessiveness and manipulative behavior.

But there was something more than her controlling manner that disturbed me. At one point, she had the nerve to suggest that Scotty and I go home and wait for her to call us when the baby was born. Throughout the course of the day, she would throw indirect nasty comments at Scotty. But surprisingly, he maintained his cool, which is usually not easy for Scotty. It was me that was actually starting to lose it. She asked him if he planned on really being involved with the baby emotionally and financially. Then she made statements, not even suggestions, about how the baby should be raised and what should be done. She even had the baby's baptism planned in a religion that wasn't even ours. Oh yes, she was dominating all right, but there was something more.

When the moment finally arrived for Chloe to have the baby, Scotty asked everyone to please leave the room. Since Chloe was having natural childbirth, he wanted to share this experience with her alone. The woman refused to leave. She was adamant in her conviction that she belonged in that room more than anyone and was not going anywhere until the baby was born. She even suggested that Scotty and I leave. Chloe had to tell her to leave and wait outside. As she stormed out the door, she proclaimed that she would be waiting right outside.

I waited a moment to wish Chloe and Scotty luck. As I left the room and walked down the hall, past the pay phones, I hear this woman talking to someone over the phone. I found out later that it was her husband.

She was telling her husband about being thrown out of the room. She said if anyone should have been thrown out of the room it should have been that dead-beat loser boyfriend and his "holier-than-thou" mother. She went on to say that no one was going to be allowed to see the baby once she got "it" home.

Well, that was about all I could stand. I started to experience feelings of rage that I hadn't felt in years. The anger I felt was spreading throughout my body. When it reached my hands, they were burning. She didn't see me until I was upon her. I grabbed the phone from her ear and slammed in down. Thankfully, I didn't strike her, although I came close. I proceeded to ask her who the hell she thought she was.

There was nothing wrong with my son wanting to be alone with his girlfriend during the birth of their baby. I said to her that she was a nothing, and that this was my granddaughter and was nothing to her. Her wide face housed two insignificant little eyes that were dressed with a pair of glasses. With those tiny eyes piercing at me she said, "That's where you're wrong; this baby is part of me, part of us."

It was with those words that I felt déjà vu. These were words that I had heard long ago. Was she implying that Eliza Jane had the "family gifts" that I had struggled with my entire life? How did she know about the "family gifts?" Then I thought, maybe I'm being paranoid.

With that thought, I yelled, "As God is my judge, you will never see or become any part of Eliza Jane's life."

Sarcastically, she said, "God? What has your God done for you? You could have had it all—powers, riches beyond your wildest dreams, fame—but no, you chose this mundane existence."

"No," I said, "I chose to share an eternity with a loving God. Your eternity with the devil will be that of eternal darkness, sorrow and misery."

She replied, "Time will tell who will be victorious. Eliza Jane will be much easier to manipulate. Although she has your gifts, she does not have your fortitude. Eliza Jane just might find what we have to offer much more appealing." With that, she scurried down the hall. This baby wasn't even born yet, and it was already starting.

When Eliza Jane was born, I was called into the room. Not wanting to alarm the new parents, I decided not to tell them what had transpired out in the hall. Actually, I did tell them about the terrible things she was saying over the phone. I just left out her comments about trying to control Eliza Jane. Those comments alone were enough to ban her from the room for good. Although that night, she called Chloe and told her that she would be up in a couple of days to take them home.

Little did she know, the very night that Eliza Jane was born, I discussed with Wayne the possibility of taking Chloe and Eliza Jane in until they found an apartment, and he agreed. Actually, I had secretly hoped that if Chloe and Scotty spent enough time together they would eventually marry.

The day it was time to take Eliza Jane home, I brought up the outfit that Scotty and Chloe had picked out. However, upon my arrival, I saw that woman out in the waiting room. She still actually thought she was going to walk out that door with Eliza Jane. Apparently, she hadn't done enough research on me. I wasn't one to ever give up.

She was stunned as she saw Wayne and I walk by her into Chloe's room. As I walked by, I did manage to stop and provide her with a victorious smirk. At that moment, I felt completely in control and powerful, almost vengeful, and that scared me. I could only imagine what I could have been like if I chose to worship and follow the devil instead of God. Nonetheless, I still enjoyed walking out the door with Eliza Jane safely in my hands.

By the time Eliza Jane was about four months old, as I speculated, Chloe and Scotty had gotten closer and decided to rent an apartment of their own and live together. It wasn't the marriage that I'd hoped for, but it was a start.

Although I didn't condone unmarried people living together, I was glad to see them living as a family. While both of them worked, my mother and I babysat during the day. Eliza Jane was like a ray of sunshine coming into the house daily. As Eliza Jane grew, my mother could not get over how much she looked and acted like me. She possessed a physical and spiritual beauty.

Although grandchildren are usually naturally close to their grandparents, Eliza Jane was unusually attached to me and her Uncle Joe. Although Wayne and my mother tried getting close to her, she seemed to only want Joe or me to hold her.

When Eliza Jane was about nine months old, she did something starling. As I was holding her and we walked past Jane's picture collage (after her death, using all my pictures, each one of the immediate family members made a collage of Jane to hang up in their homes) Eliza Jane started crying and pointing to it. When we walked over to the picture collage, Eliza Jane immediately pointed out Jane in the picture and looked at me. I told her that it was Aunt Jane. And although other people were included in each picture of Jane, she would only point out Jane and look at me, waiting for my response. This became an everyday event. It got to the point where I didn't want to walk by the collage. What I didn't understand is that I had another picture collage of myself, Wayne and the kids when they were little. Eliza Jane wasn't interested in that collage at all.

Months went by, and one day, as we walked by the picture collage, she cried to see it, as usual. But this time, she did something amazing. When Eliza Jane pointed out Jane in the picture, instead of waiting for my response, she proceeded to point to herself and say, "Me."

Eliza Jane had never said the word "me" before, and was just barely saying "Mama." At first, I thought it was merely a coincidence. But once again, she pointed at Jane, then pointed to herself and in a loud voice, clearly stated the word, "Me."

I was astounded. As a Catholic, I do not believe in reincarnation. There's no point to it. Why would God want to recycle a used soul? If not reincarnation, what was this message Eliza Jane was trying to communicate? I do believe that infants, such as Eliza Jane, can see spirits and listen to the dead. I have believed from the day Jane died that her spirit wanders through my house. I believe this primarily because Joe lives with us. Jane was always so concerned about dying and leaving Joe that I don't know if she has actually ever left him.

I am speculating that Eliza Jane has seen Jane, who has spoken to her. Why did Jane choose Eliza Jane? Well, besides Eliza Jane being Jane's namesake, if she does possess special powers, Eliza Jane would be the perfect candidate with whom to communicate.

Was this the reason why Eliza Jane continues to be so attached to Joe and me? When Jane was alive, she was also extremely close to both of us. The pieces seemed to fit too precisely, although I still didn't fully understand Eliza Jane's connection to Jane. Just as we were getting used to babysitting and caring for Eliza Jane, along came another surprise.

It was Halloween that Chloe found out that she was pregnant again. After going to the doctor's, Chloe found out that she was due in December. I know you're wondering how a woman can't know that she is seven months pregnant. My thoughts were that she was in denial, because Chloe genuinely seemed like she was in shock when she found out.

Because she was so far along, the hospital decided to do an ultrasound to determine if pregnancy was progressing satisfactorily. When the ultrasound was conducted, they found out that Chloe was having a boy. The baby was to be Scotty's first boy and our first grandson. Unfortunately, the ultra sound also revealed that he was a breech baby and a c-section would be required.

It was right before Thanksgiving when Chloe came home from work, as usual, and started telling me about her day. Chloe said that she had a strange sensation and all this water came gushing out. Well, Chloe's water never broke with Eliza Jane, so she really didn't know what was happening, but I did. I knew that if Chloe didn't get to the hospital right away, there could be severe problems.

Scotty was at a business meeting about an hour away, so Wayne and I took Chloe to the hospital. Scotty arrived within the hour and an emergency c-section was performed. Although premature, the baby was just fine. However, he would need to stay in the Newborn ICU for awhile.

In spite of the adverse conditions, baby Scotty endured. Yes, the baby was named Scotty Mendes IV. As Scotty stayed in the room with Chloe, Wayne and I sat out in the waiting room in hopes that we would have an opportunity to see the baby. As I sat there pondering the situation in the waiting room, it suddenly hit me, Today was November 22, my sister Jane's birthday. Between Eliza Jane and baby Scotty, what message was being delivered to me?

Baby Scotty came home from the hospital on Thanksgiving Day. As he grew, I would find him to be much different than Eliza Jane. Initially, Baby Scotty seemed to be much more happy and carefree. He was always smiling. He also didn't look anything like Eliza Jane. Baby Scotty was showing all the signs of having red hair, just like his grandfather, Scott.

What really gave me the chills was when his dark blue, oval-shaped eyes turned a light robin's-egg blue. This was the exact color of my dead ex-mother-in-law's eyes. For some reason, baby Scotty didn't seem as close to me as Eliza Jane. He usually tries to push himself away from me unless he wants to be picked up or fed. It was also right around the time Scotty was nine months old that he also cried to see the pictures of Jane. Like Eliza Jane, Scotty pointed to Jane and looked at me.

After much reflection and meditation, I have come to conclude that this is God's way of letting me know that Jane's spirit is alive and well. Baby Scotty being born on Jane's birthday signified "new birth." Although Jane is my sister, her blood also courses through the veins of my grandchildren, including Eliza Jane.

The following June after Baby Scotty's birth, Scotty and Chloe were finally married. Today, as the end of October nears and the Halloween season is right around the corner, I sit here reflecting the events that have occurred over the past twenty-five years.

Although Scotty seems to be living a structured, calmer life, I can't help but feel he was manipulated by the devil at some points, directly or indirectly. Scotty will spend countless hours reading about vampires and the supernatural, and he doesn't find even one hour to go to church. Not that this makes anyone evil, but Scotty's infant experiences were not that of your normal baby.

Was Scotty actually impacted on that fateful day so long ago when the devil and his disciples appeared to us? If so, this only means that Scotty will be forced to fight harder against the devil though out his life.

Based on that woman's comments in the hospital, it is obvious to me that Eliza Jane will need to be carefully monitored and mentored appropriately. For Eliza Jane has inherited the "family gift." However, does this this mean that Baby Scotty, Felicity and any other of my grandchildren will be spared? Possibly not! Our ancestors said that there would be "one" in every generation. No one ever said there couldn't be more than one.

Also, there are other family members. What about them and their children? Well, I do know of their stories, but you'll have to wait for the next book to come out. Some of their stories are more amazing than mine. Some of them are uncannily familiar.

However, the big question is whether other family members, their children, my children and my grandchildren will have the ability and insight to decipher good people and actions verses evil. If so, what choices will they make?

What about me? Have the demonic attempts to obtain my soul ended?

Well, in June of 2002, we decided to move back home to Rhode Island. Scotty, Chloe, Eliza Jane and Baby Scotty had moved back a year earlier. Therefore, I am back, back where it all began. While in Virginia, Wayne and I had my sister-in-law, who is a realtor, look for a house for us. Although it is difficult to find any available land in Rhode Island, my sister-in-law somehow knew a builder who was building a new house on some wooded property at the top of a hill. After looking at some pictures, we told her to proceed. We ended up moving in at the end of August 2002. Although the house is just beautiful, it's kind of eerie at the same time. We are sitting on top of a hill, surrounded by woods. Actually, the woods come right up to our bedroom window. After living there only a week, I was sure my new adventures would soon begin.

It was just last night that I awoke to the sound of a loud owl screeching at my window. Believe it or not, I had never actually heard an owl before. But that wasn't what scared me. Each time the owl screeched, someone from inside my house replied back. It was almost as if they were communicating with each other.

When I looked over at Wayne, he was sleeping. I walked over to my bedroom window, opened it and looked outside. I could not find the owl. I shut the window and proceeded to walk down the hall to my mother's, Joe's and Wayne II's bedrooms. As I peeked inside each room, everyone appeared to be deeply sleeping.

After that task was completed, I walked back into my room and jumped back in bed. Within the next several minutes, the loud owl call was back. Once more, a reply came from inside my house. This went on for at least an hour. I finally fell back to sleep.

However, today I asked everyone about the owl, and no one knew what I was talking about. You may ask, what's the big deal about seeing an owl? Well Portuguese believe that a death in the family will occur to the person who hears an owl that no one else does. Who was that someone in my house who was communicating with the owl? I'm sure no one I know above ground.

Unfortunately, there is still much evil that surrounds me. The one thing I have come to realize is that although I might have the opportunity to become a "Portuguese Witch," I have chosen not to. If it hadn't been for my extremely religious family, I might have made a different choice. I thank them for their guidance, especially my grandparents and mother.

I have been fortunate enough to recognize God's gift of free will. For as powerful as the devil may appear to be, God's powers are infinite. Each time I prophesize, see spirits, have out-of-body experiences and see other spiritual dimensions, I know those gifts are gifts from God, and not the devil. The devil merely wants to utilize and abuse these gifts for his own destructive purposes. I can only pray that my family and grandchildren use their own gifts with special care.

As for me, I will continue to be watchful and aware, and will in my own way defeat some of the evil that surrounds us all. Hopefully, you'll hear from me in the near future, with the upcoming sequel to this book—that is, if the owl's appearance wasn't foreshadowing my own death.

I am hopeful that it wasn't, because only days later after I wrote that line, as I was walking down my front stairs carrying a bag of clothes I had put together for the veterans, I once again felt both feet slip off the top step of the stairs. And once again, my guardian angel carefully placed me back on the top step with bag in hand. I wasn't so surprised this time.

But I was surprised days later when my mother, while cleaning out her curio cabinet, pulled out a small porcelain doll. It looked familiar, but I couldn't remember where my mother had gotten it. When I asked my mother about it she said that Scott had given it to her along time ago. He told her it was part of his mother's collection. He had offered it to you but you didn't want it so he gave it to me.

My mother didn't realize the truth in that statement. He "gave" it to all us all right—whether intentionally or not. Could all the additional evil experienced throughout the years be because of that doll? I guess I'll find out someday.

However, for now, it did make me realize that my mission on this earth was not through. Who knows what evil and good experiences lay ahead for this would-be Feiteceira?

By the way, our cousin Christopher died suddenly this week. I guess the owl superstition is true.

0-595-27006-9